ACCEPT TH

CUZ THER

ONE WAY 2 PLAY!

FEATURING

DAVID ROBINSON

BETSY KING

BRENT JONES

TOM LANDRY

AND OTHERS!

DAL SHEALY & PAT SPRINGLE

THOMAS NELSON PUBLISHERS
Nashville

Copyright © 1995 by Fellowship of Christian Athletes

Published in Nashville, Tennessee, by Thomas Nelson, Inc., Publishers, and distributed in Canada by Word Communications, Ltd., Richmond, British Columbia, and in the United Kingdom by Word (UK), Ltd., Milton Keynes, England.

Scripture quotations are from the NEW KING JAMES VERSION of the Bible. Copyright © 1979, 1980, 1982, Thomas Nelson, Inc., Publishers.

Library of Congress Cataloging-in-Publication Data

Shealy, Dal.
    One way 2 play / Dal Shealy and Pat Springle.
        p.   cm.
    Includes bibliographical references.
    ISBN 0-7852-7676-9 (pbk. : alk. paper)
    1. Church work with teenagers—United States. 2. Teenagers—United States—Religious life. 3. Teenagers—Drug use. 4. Teenagers—Alcohol use. 5. Sports—Religious aspects—Christianity. 6. Fellowship of Christian Athletes. 7. Athletes—United States—Interviews. 8. Athletes—United States—Religious life. I. Springle, Pat, 1950–
BV4447.S49 1995
259'.23—dc20   95-8014
                                                  CIP

Printed in the United States of America

1 2 3 4 5 6 7 - 01 00 99 98 97 96 95

DEDICATION

We dedicate this book to Tom Landry, a godly man who exemplifies faith, courage, and commitment. Coach Landry's consistent lifestyle, faithful service to the Fellowship of Christian Athletes, and tender heart have touched the lives of athletes, coaches, and parents for thirty-five years. By his example, he has demonstrated the true One Way 2 Play!

CONTENTS

PREFACE

Dear Friend,

Early in my coaching career, two realities became clear to me, and they changed the way I coached. One, I was moved by the impact I had on my players. And two, I noticed the impact that sports had on our community. These two realities brought into perspective the importance of my responsibility as a coach, and they are the reasons I am excited to tell you about a Fellowship of Christian Athletes program that will help you make a positive impact.

In a recent survey of 125,000 coaches, over 90 percent told us that the number-one challenge they face in dealing with their athletes is the problem of drug and alcohol use. The Fellowship of Christian Athletes's One Way 2 Play—Drug Free! is an awareness, education, prevention, and recovery program that is geared to help students understand some basic truths about drugs and alcohol, make the choice not to use them, and set up positive peer pressure to help support their choice.

The encouragement to make good, godly decisions about alcohol and drugs is communicated most powerfully in groups. Fellowship of Christian Athletes groups are called Huddles, and they blend fun, fellowship, teaching, and accountability to help young men and women live for Christ.

This book provides the information you need to help your group remain drug- and alcohol-free. In these pages, you will find:

- information on why students use drugs; how to tell if students are using; responsibilities of the coach, parent, team, and student; and how to set up positive peer pressure

- interviews with top athletes and coaches
- outlines for two meetings that will help you to implement this program with your team, Huddle, campus club, or youth group
- a list of additional resources available to help you promote One Way 2 Play—Drug Free! within your group

I think you will find One Way 2 Play—Drug Free! to be a valuable tool. I only wish there had been a similar tool to help me during my twenty-seven years of coaching.

Sincerely,
Dal Shealy, President
Fellowship of Christian
Athletes

ONE WAY 2 PLAY—DRUG FREE! AN OVERVIEW

One Way 2 Play—Drug Free! draws on the expertise of Christians in the field of alcohol and drug education, prevention, and recovery. With their input, we have created a program which God can use to touch young lives. One Way 2 Play—Drug Free! is innovative, relevant, and effective.

This exciting program includes:

- this book, which provides important information about the effect of drugs and alcohol on the lives of young people, presents testimonies from athletes, and lists practical steps to help young people live for Christ, drug- and alcohol-free.
- four simple implementation steps to help you use this program effectively in your youth group or team (Appendix B).
- plans for two group meetings to help you communicate the message of One Way 2 Play—Drug Free! (Appendix B).
- One Way 2 Play—Drug Free! commitment sheets, which provide opportunities for students to state their intention to live and play drug-free (Appendix B).
- hats, pins, posters, bumper stickers, and other items to reinforce the message of One Way 2 Play—Drug Free! (An order form is included in the back of this book.)
- a recognizable accountability sign (the One Way 2 Play—Drug Free! hand signal of a raised index finger, just like the hand signal printed on the commitment sheet), which reminds teens to be strong when in the face of temptation.

- a team of professionals who are willing and able to help counsel you when needs arise in discussions about drugs and alcohol. (Rapha Treatment Centers, one of the nation's largest providers of psychiatric and substance abuse treatment programs from a distinctively Christian perspective, can be reached at 1-800-383-HOPE.)

If you have any questions about how you can use One Way 2 Play!, please call or write our national office:

Fellowship of Christian Athletes
8701 Leeds Road
Kansas City, MO 64129-1680
816-289-0909

INTRODUCTION

A recent Gallup Poll found that coaches consider drug and alcohol abuse a significant problem on their campuses. Seventy-nine percent of coaches believe alcohol is hurting students, and 66 percent see tobacco use as a problem. The good news from this survey is that three-fourths of the coaches report their schools have programs to help students deal with substance abuse problems. Over one-fourth have initiated their own programs. The poll states:

> Beyond the stereotype of the high school gym teacher who just shows films in health class, these coaches are actively engaged in counseling student athletes, meeting with their parents or guardians, and conducting special classes for students or their fellow coaches. Also, two coaches in three say they specifically discuss the problems of substance abuse at pre-season meetings with student team members, and sometimes with their parents. . . . Nearly half of the coaches say they would like to receive special training to deal with the drug problem.

One Way 2 Play—Drug Free! is specifically designed for these coaches, student leaders, parents, and school officials. The problem—and the solution—reaches beyond student athletes to every segment of the culture. We watch the evening news and see teenage gangs killing each other over dope . . . or a pair of tennis shoes. We read in the paper about a drunk seventeen-year-old who smashes his car into a family of six, killing three of them. We look at the strange clothes and rings in the noses and tongues of teenagers on the way to school, and we wonder, "What's going on with them? Why are they so weird?" And these are only the most obvious and identifiable signs of a youth culture in trouble.

Under the best of circumstances, adolescence is a difficult time in a person's life. Monumental physical, emotional, and relational changes occur during this time. Children are becoming adults, and in the process, they try lots of new behaviors. Some are helpful; some are very destructive.

In addition to the normal developmental changes of adolescence, today's young people experience many other pressures. Families are falling apart. In inner cities, traditional families rarely exist at all. Responsible role models have been replaced by wealthy sports and movie stars, and young people have unrealistic expectations about what they deserve and need.

Many young people long for escape and a sense of belonging. The gangs we see on the evening news are only one example. Suburban middle- and upper-middle-class students escape more quietly but in far greater numbers. Some seek to escape in emotion-numbing drugs and alcohol.

Today, many young people feel lonely. They feel hopeless, and they desperately need somebody to reach out to them. Your church youth group, Young Life, Youth for Christ, Student Venture, Athletes in Action, or Fellowship of Christian Athletes Huddle can be a place where teens feel understood and loved, and where they can get direction in making wise decisions about their lives. You have the privilege of letting God use you to address the causes, as well as the symptoms, of teen drug use. You play a vital role in shaping young lives so that they—and eventually their children—feel loved and make responsible, healthy decisions.

One Way 2 Play—Drug Free! is the Fellowship of Christian Athletes's program to confront the problem of drug use. It goes far beyond "Just Say No!" campaigns, because it helps you create a powerful, healthy atmosphere and provides clear information and guidance for young people. We address the entire scope of teens' lives, not just one behavior. This comprehensive approach takes longer to communicate and more care to implement, but the quality of relationships which are built will be the basis for healthy communication and changed lives.

1

THE PRESSURE COOKER

San Antonio Spurs All-Star center David Robinson is known for excellence on and off the court. His attitude while he's playing—and his lifestyle in general—reflect integrity. In a world where it sometimes seems everyone is going in the same direction, Robinson is setting a clearly different and higher standard: to follow Christ. His faith, character, and ability have won the admiration of coaches, players, and fans. David's relationship with Christ gives him a sense of purpose and a clear focus so he can perform up to his immense abilities—with a blend of intensity and grace. David Robinson is a true Christian gentleman. . . with an awesome slam!

David Robinson

NBA All-Star center for the San Antonio Spurs

I have never, ever been tempted in the least to use drugs or alcohol. I saw what it did to other people, and I didn't want that to happen to me. I sure didn't want to drink when I was down because I knew it would only make things worse.

I never hung out with people who drank or did drugs. I was focused on playing well. Of course, I heard and read about athletes who got in trouble, but I had developed such an aversion to drinking, drugs, and smoking that these things didn't attract me at all.

My mother was a Christian, but I never really received her message. Then, when I got into the NBA, I suddenly had everything people could ever want. I had all the success, but it didn't give me a sense of stability and peace. At times, things would be going great. The fans cheered, but boy, you feel really low when the fans aren't cheering and people are talking about you like you're a dog! My emotions were too locked in on people's approval and on failure and success. But I didn't draw those lines for failure and success. The media did. It was like chasing your tail. I realized that I was doing pretty well, but then I looked at a guy like Michael Jordan who had a championship ring and made a little more money than me. Then I saw him on TV kissing a trophy! Then they told him that one championship wasn't enough. Magic has five! It's really sad. No matter how much money you're making or how well you're playing, they always raise the stakes on you. The world sets that standard, and when you meet it, they raise it higher every time. They're never satisfied with what you accomplish, so consequently, you're never satisfied with what you accomplish. That's why they call it "the rat race"!

Through thinking about all this, I realized that all I was pursuing couldn't fulfill me. I was a successful athlete making a lot of money, but if I couldn't be happy with myself, something was wrong! Ninety-nine percent of the people in the world would want to be in my shoes, but I was still looking for more. That's what shocked me into waking up! What I had should be plenty, but no matter how much you have, it doesn't seem like enough because these things can't satisfy your deepest needs. That's when I realized I needed the Lord.

Back in 1986, at the World Championships, I had the same creepy feeling. I felt unstable. On the plane on the way back from Amsterdam, an evangelist talked to us about Christ. I prayed with him, but I didn't understand what I was doing. It sounded good, but I just didn't get it. For the next five years, I knew there had to be more to this Christianity stuff than this! I called myself a Christian because I had prayed with this guy, but Christ hadn't become real to me at that point. In the back of my mind, I knew there had to be more.

On June 8, 1991, a minister came to San Antonio from Austin. He was with a group called Champions for Christ. He and I talked, and he asked me some questions. The first question he asked was, "David, do you love God?"

I was a little surprised, and I said, "Well, of course I love God."

Then he asked, "How much time do you spend praying?"

I said, "Every once in a while. I eat three times a day, and I pray then!"

Then he asked me, "How much time do you spend reading your Bible?"

I answered, "There's one around here somewhere. I've got one. I just don't understand it. It doesn't make a lot of sense to me."

He said, "When you love someone, don't you usually take time to get to know them? Don't you want to know them better?"

To be honest, when he said that, the first thing I thought was, "Well, God is not a real person." But that day, Christ became a real person to me.

He asked me one more question. He said, "The Old Testament says to set aside one day a week to honor God. When was the last time you spent one day——not one day a week, just one day——to praise God and thank Him for what you have?"

I realized I had never given God a day to praise and thank Him. I felt like a spoiled brat! Everything was about me, me, me, me, me. How much more money can I make? It was all about David's praise and David's glory. Everybody cheering David. Everybody patting David on the back. I had never stopped to honor God for all He had done for me. That really hit me, and I just cried. I cried all afternoon, and I prayed and told the Lord, "Everything You've given me I'm giving back to You today!" That was a big moment in my life.

I see the effects of drugs and alcohol on people's lives, and I'm glad I never got into it. My life wouldn't be nearly as prosperous. Young people, wake up and see the effects of alcohol and drugs on other people! What makes you think you are different or stronger than the next guy, and that it's not going to hurt you? Don't be stupid! Don't think you're strong enough. You're not! You need the foundation of Christ in your life to help you be strong and wise enough to make good decisions. Drugs and alcohol are a big problem in our society. They show our main weakness: ourselves, our sinfulness, our wrong desires.

Without Christ, you won't have the foundation to resist temptations. You're going to be arrogant and self-centered. Without Christ, you won't be able to resist all this. It's too powerful. Find out what is really important. Find out that God is real, and trust Him.

Coach Martin had noticed that Jim's performance was beginning to slip over the past week of two-a-days. Then, about halfway through an afternoon practice, Jim missed an easy block on the outside linebacker. The back got clobbered! And when he got up, he must have said something to Jim because in an instant, Jim threw a punch.

The rest of the players and the coaches got them cooled down, and practice continued. When it was over, Jim slowly meandered to the locker room by himself. Coach Martin found him there.

"How's it going, son?" He put his arm around the boy's shoulder.

Jim looked down. "Okay, I guess."

"Yeah, you're doing okay, but it seems like something's on your mind. Anything eating at you?"

Jim got defensive. "I said I'm okay, Coach!"

Then Jim realized his response had been a little hot. "Sorry, Coach. I guess . . . well, I guess my mind just isn't on the game these days. I'll try to do better."

Jim was new to town and to the team. Coach Martin knew little about the boy except that his parents were divorced and that he seemed to be a pretty good fullback. It was late. Both of them were tired and hot. But Martin decided to probe a little.

"Jim, your parents are divorced, aren't they?" Jim nodded but didn't say anything. Coach Martin continued.

"Where's your dad right now?"

"He's somewhere in California, working on an oil pipeline. I haven't seen him in a while."

Coach Martin was encouraged by this crack in the door of information, so he asked another question. "I'll bet it's hard to come in here from another town and another team and start over, isn't it?"

"Yeah," Jim sighed heavily. "It's real hard." He paused, then said, "We left my sister back in Ohio to have a baby."

"That's great!" Coach Martin said.

"It's not that great!" Jim said disgustedly. "She's not married, and my mom is really hacked off at her." He paused again, then looked at the coach.

"I know I've messed up a lot lately, Coach Martin, but I'm really mad at my dad for leaving, my sister for being so stupid, and my mom for being so mad all the time."

Coach Martin felt compassion for the boy. "Why didn't you tell me, Jim? I'd like to help you if I can."

Jim replied, "Oh, I don't know. I guess everybody has problems like this, don't they, Coach?"

The world young people live in today is very different from the one their coaches and parents experienced. Why?

One, the pace of life is much faster. Take a look at a few old movies and note the difference between their snail's-paced plots and the rapid-fire action of *Terminator II*.

Two, we are far more mobile today than we were a couple of decades ago. The average person today moves seven times in his or her lifetime. Only a few years ago, most people stayed in the same community their whole lives.

Three, we are bombarded by an incredible amount of information. Living in the "information age" provides us with instant access to news and world developments. We have access to hundreds of cable stations that suit any and every taste in information and entertainment.

Four, personal initiative is slowly being eroded. We expect our government, family, or friends to fix every problem. And the "welfare state" is not the only example. We also blame others for our problems instead of having the courage and tenacity to make necessary changes. We have become, as one writer put it, "a nation of victims."

The fragmentation of families, the disorientation caused by mobility, the glut of information, and our feelings of victimization make this the toughest time in history to be a young person.

Some coaches and parents try to motivate teenagers by saying, "When I was your age . . ." followed by an account of their problems and exploits. But the problem is that today is different—*really* different—from "when I was your age." A recent survey demonstrates the stark contrast between the environment and stress levels of young people today and those of three decades ago. Thirty years ago, teachers were asked the question: "What are the biggest problems in school?" Their top five responses were:

1. chewing gum in class
2. not putting trash in the trash can
3. using bad language
4. dressing inappropriately
5. cheating

Today's teachers would be glad to have such minor problems! When asked the same question, they listed their top five problems as:

1. drug abuse
2. teen pregnancy and sexual diseases
3. vandalism
4. gangs/aggressive and assaultive behavior
5. stealing[1]

Young people desperately need love and stability. But their world seldom provides these necessities. Charles Colson commented on the lack of purpose and meaning in the youth culture in his book *Against the Night.*

> Fragmented families and rootless youth are not confined to the inner city, of course. The crisis reaches every part of our society. Who hasn't seen the packs of mall orphans cruising shopping centers to avoid returning to homes shattered by divorce, neglect, or abuse? Each year about two million young people between the ages of thirteen and nineteen attempt suicide....What drives our youth to such horrifying lengths? Morally impoverished, groping for love and direction, the children find evil substitutes in all the wrong places.[2]

The "evil substitutes" are often drugs and alcohol, which play a major role in teenagers' desire to escape. Suicide is the ultimate escape. The American Council for Drug Education reports that more than 70 percent of teenagers who attempt suicide used alcohol or drugs frequently.[3] But there are many others. Some teens try to compensate for their pain by being successful in sports, academics, or social settings. Others develop addictions to sex, food, or work. Still others use drugs or alcohol to blunt the pain they feel.

In his insightful book *In One Day: The Things Americans Do in a Day,* Tom Parker lists a few of our favorite escape mechanisms. Every day, Americans:

- drink 15.7 million gallons of beer—about 28 million six-packs
- drink 1.2 million gallons of liquor
- take 30 million sleeping pills
- smoke 85,000 pounds of marijuana
- snort 325 pounds of cocaine[4]

"But these statistics are for the general population," you may say. True, but the statistics for youth are equally alarming.

- Of the fifteen million alcoholics in this country, four million are under eighteen.

- The first drink generally occurs at age twelve.
- Ten- and twelve-year-old alcoholics and addicts are no longer rare.
- The number of high school students who are intoxicated at least once a month has more than doubled since 1986. One survey reported that 11 percent of these students were alcoholics.
- Alcohol-related deaths on the highways are the number-one killer of people aged fifteen to twenty-four.
- The long-established trend of lower drug use among youth is reversing.[5]

Younger children also experience intense peer pressure to drink and use drugs. By the fourth grade:

- 40 percent feel pressured by friends to smoke cigarettes
- 34 percent feel pressured to drink wine coolers
- 24 percent say their friends encourage them to use cocaine or crack[6]

The statistics for Christian teenagers are almost the same as for unchurched young people. A few years ago, Josh McDowell's ground-breaking book *Why Wait?* stated that Christians participated in premarital sex only 10 percent less frequently than non-Christians.[7] The statistics on drugs and alcohol echo that sad finding. A Gallup Poll reported that 80 percent of Christian youths drink beer, lagging behind the 88 percent of non-Christian teens who drink. Fifty-eight percent of Christian teens smoke tobacco; 65 percent of non-Christians smoke. But surprisingly, Christian students actually surpass nonbelievers in marijuana use: 47 percent of Christians smoke pot, as opposed to 38 percent of non-Christians.[8]

The pressures on young Christians are virtually the same as those on their classmates, and they succumb to those pressures almost as often. But parents, coaches, and youth ministers don't want to admit that drug use is prevalent among Christian youth. So both groups, young people and adults, pretend the problem doesn't exist.

Sports can be a big part of the solution to this problem. Athletics builds responsibility and teamwork and provides positive, constructive outlets for youthful energies. But sports can be a part of the problem too. Parents and coaches who push young people too hard create stress and tear down self-esteem and responsibility instead of building them. And sports can be one of the areas in which unrealistic expectations warp perspective. Every kid in America wants to "be like Mike" and flash that winning smile along with those winning moves. The Nike commercials look like a lot of fun, but what happens when the hopes and dreams of being a superstar are shattered by a missed block or a bad shot? Will there be a friend or a parent who will say, "That's okay. You're still the greatest to me"? Will there be a coach like Georgetown University basketball coach John Thompson, who hugged his player after he lost the ball on the final, critical play in the national championship game?

Young people have plenty of stress in their lives today. Perhaps the greatest gift we can give them is to help them develop skills to handle that stress effectively. That may be even more important than good pass-blocking or a good jump shot!

2

SO WHAT'S THE DEAL?

Tom Landry
Former head coach of the Dallas Cowboys

Years ago, an outstanding young player joined the Cowboys as a rookie. It looked like he was going to have a tremendous career, but after that first season, he got in with the wrong crowd. When he came back to training camp the next year, he definitely was on drugs. There wasn't any question about it.

This player's life changed noticeably during that second year. He was like Dr. Jekyll and Mr. Hyde. One day he would come into the dressing room, and he would be very cordial, saying "Hello." to one of his buddies. But the next day, his buddy might speak to him, and he would turn and snap, "Hey, man, I don't want to hear that!" He ignored coaches and players. He stopped paying attention to us. Strangely, his play wasn't as affected by his drug use as you might expect. He could go onto the practice field or to a game, and though he appeared not to be paying attention, he made very few mistakes. We won the Super Bowl that year with him, but the next year, he became very distant to both the coaching staff and the players. He was using drugs even more at that point, and his behavior became so disruptive, we realized we couldn't even keep him on our team. It was tragic to me: a gifted player whose career—whose life—was being destroyed by drugs.

He was traded from club to club, but unfortunately, this young man was never the player he could have been. He was never a very good player after that first year. After he quit playing, he overcame his drug problem. Years later when I spoke at an FCA function, he came to see me, and he told me that he had changed the direction of his life. I was very glad to hear that because I really liked him. He was a very likable and good man when he wasn't on drugs.

Most players hide their use of drugs. Our coaching staff learned to recognize players' use of drugs, and it became very noticeable if they were taking them. Early in my coaching career, if I called a player in to confront him, he would say, "Coach, I'm not using them," even though it was very evident he was taking some kind of drug. Later, more players were willing to admit they had problems so they could get some help. It takes a lot of courage to say, "Coach, I've got a problem."

Sometimes a player might come to me to tell me another player was having a problem with drinking. The players really tried to help each other, not so much because it was hurting the team—even though it probably did. They got involved because they cared about each other. When we care about other people, we do whatever it takes to help them out.

I never had a desire to use drugs or alcohol because I knew it would hurt my abilities as a football player and hinder my future in football. I don't think there's any question about it: When you start drinking or using drugs, you never know if you're going to become an addict. Sometimes a player can try it just once and become addicted very quickly. Even when it takes much longer, it still devastates lives. I saw some of my good friends just out of college who were drinking, and I saw them later when the alcohol had destroyed their lives. It was sad to see. I hated to see how they had been affected.

If you use alcohol or drugs, you'll never achieve the goals you want to achieve. I strongly encourage young people not to drink or use drugs because if they do, they won't be able to take advantage of the opportunities this great country offers.

When you accept Christ as your Lord and Savior, he will direct you away from drugs and alcohol. I've seen many players come to Christ, and when they did, they had a new sense of purpose in life. They no longer needed substances to fill the emptiness in their lives. Christ did that for them.

"It's so stupid for Billy to use that stuff!" Sarah told a friend in disgust. "Can't he see that he's ruining his life?"

The answer to that question was obvious to Sarah, but it isn't clear to someone who abuses alcohol or drugs. In fact, our behavior almost always seems logical to us, even if to others it is clearly destructive. There are many reasons people *start* drinking or using, but they *continue* to drink or use because it seems like a viable solution to the stress they feel. To them, it works: "I don't drink because I like the taste," one girl said. "I drink to get drunk—so I can forget."

The use of drugs, especially alcohol, is epidemic in our country. By their senior year in high school, two out of three students are alcohol drinkers. One in twenty drinks daily, and nearly four out of ten consume five or more drinks in a row at least every two weeks.[1]

There are several reasons young people start down this destructive path:

- the desire to experiment with something new and exciting
- the desire to escape emotional pain
- the desire to blunt anger

- the desire to fit in with peers
- parental modeling

Let's examine each of these reasons.

EXPERIMENTATION

Most young people have their first joint or beer because they've seen older kids and adults doing it, and it looks like fun. Television commercials portray happy, healthy young people drinking beer and enjoying an ideal—and usually an athletic—lifestyle. This illusion is pervasive and powerful. In fact, it is estimated that an average eighteen-year-old has seen 100,000 beer commercials, all designed by slick ad executives to entice young people to drink.[2]

These alluring images coincide with the normal adolescent urge to try new things, push beyond the boundaries, and dabble in things taboo. Teens feel a rush of adrenaline when they drink their first beer or smoke their first joint, and their courage to experiment is often rewarded with instant acceptance by their peers.

Adolescence is an age of experimentation. As one youth pastor put it, "It's their *job* to try new things!" The problem today is that the range of possible choices is much greater, and the consequences are often more dangerous. Stupid stunts have always been common to teenagers, but recently these stunts have become increasingly deadly. Not long ago, several teenagers were killed or disabled when they lay down on a highway to experience the thrill of letting cars and trucks zoom around them. They had seen this stunt in a movie.

In deteriorating families, teens don't get the good modeling and wisdom they need. Instead, the role models that shape their experimentation are movie characters and peers—hardly sources of profound wisdom!

ESCAPING EMOTIONAL PAIN

The family is a person's greatest source of strength, love, and wisdom. When that vital environment is shaken, however, family members experience the opposite of those benefits: weakness, bitterness, and confusion. Individual responses vary widely. For instance, some people withdraw so they won't get hurt again. Some attempt to dominate others so they can feel superior. Some try to gain approval by fixing other people's problems. Some try to control their lives and environments by being perfectionists. All of these wounded people are trying to deal with unresolved emotional pain.

We call these families "dysfunctional," but we shouldn't make the mistake of believing that all families are dysfunctional or that functional families don't have problems. Functional families have their share of problems, but they adapt to meet the needs and work through the difficulties. Family members come out stronger as a result of this process. In contrast, dysfunctional families focus their energies on placing blame instead of on finding solutions. They don't seek creative solutions to problems; they give up in hopelessness. The pain continues to fester as new wounds are inflicted, and each family member tries to block the pain and find some sense of meaning in life.

Statistics give us a glimpse of the depth and breadth of hurt in people's lives, but raw numbers can't begin to tell of the emotional devastation they represent.

- Approximately thirty million Americans are chemically dependent.
- Twelve million Americans are compulsive gamblers.
- Twelve million are workaholics.
- Forty to eighty million are compulsive overeaters.
- Reports of sexual abuse increased from six thousand in 1976 to two hundred thousand in 1988.
- Every addict or abuser affects at least four other people.
- In many inner cities, the illegitimacy rate is 80 percent.
- Among all whites, the illegitimacy rate is now 24 percent.
- Suicides among young people age fifteen to nineteen have almost tripled since 1960.
- Half of all marriages end in divorce.
- Twenty-six percent of all children live in single-parent homes.
- Thirty-five percent of all children live in stepfamilies.[3]

Parents in these families are often overwhelmed with their own problems, and they cannot (or will not) give the time and energy necessary to provide love and direction for their children. One woman's statement is indicative: "This kid is just too much trouble. I've got enough trouble of my own without having to tend to his too! He's got friends. He'll make it." Others are more compassionate but no more effective: "I've tried everything I can to get through to my daughter, but I've got to go to work to make a living for her and her two brothers. I can't be everywhere at once!"

Stress has many different effects on people. Its physiological effects include headaches, ulcers and other stomach problems, and a variety of psychosomatic illnesses. Stress also inhibits the body's immune system and makes it more susceptible to disease. The emotional effects of stress include anger, depression, and emotional numbness. The social effects of stress include aggressiveness, excessive shyness, and risk avoidance. Behavioral problems that result from stress include alcohol and drug abuse, truancy, and vandalism.

Adolescence is hard enough under the best of circumstances, but when there is little love, little time, and poor parental modeling, the pain is compounded. Typical responses to the weight of this pain are to:

- *minimize*: "Oh, it isn't that big of a deal. It doesn't hurt much. I can handle it."
- *deny*: "Nah, that doesn't affect me at all. I don't even know what you're talking about!"
- *internalize*: "My parents divorced because I'm a bad person. I'm the one to blame."
- *externalize*: "Okay, so I stole something. So what? If my parents loved me, I wouldn't do stuff like that. It's their fault!"

Some people respond to intense, unresolved pain by becoming emotionally numb. They don't feel pain; they don't feel joy either. Some become depressed because their unresolved hurt overwhelms their emotional and physiological functions. Whatever the response, these hurts also produce another emotion: anger.

ANGER

This emotion is so pervasive in the youth culture that many observers call this "the age of rage." Though many Christians have difficulty acknowledging anger, this feeling is a normal response to hurt and injustice. In Ephesians 4:26, Paul encouraged believers to be angry but avoid sin. The way we respond to the feeling of anger, then, can be either healthy or unhealthy, right or wrong.

Some of the causes of anger include:

Injustice   Some Christians think that anger is only justified in cases of "righteous indignation" over issues such as abortion, rape, and murder. Injustice is far broader than this. When others treat us with disrespect or ridicule us, we experience injustice, and a measure of anger is appropriate. This feeling, however, should prompt us to act appropriately, communicate with the person, and forgive the offense.

In adolescence, injustice is experienced almost every day. Teens can be vicious in their ability to inflict wounds on each other. The effects of these wounds are multiplied when young people (and adults) perceive more injustice than actually exists. When people have experienced abandonment and abuse, they tend to perceive it even when it isn't there. They feel hurt even when there is no obvious and immediate cause of that hurt, and their anger continues to build.

Pervasive Hurt   Some young people have experienced constant hurt from abandonment or physical, verbal, or sexual abuse. They have never known safety and love, so they don't even know where to look for a supportive environment. For these people, anger is a way of life.

Poor Modeling   Studies show that violent teenagers tend to come from violent homes. They have seen their parents handle stress by exploding, blaming, or withdrawing, and this response is then reenacted in their own reaction to problems. The media also provides poor modeling. Recently, attempts have been made to reduce the level of violence in movies and on television, but these efforts may only slightly reverse the trend. There are still hundreds of thousands of on-screen murders, fights, rapes, and other expressions of outrage to fill teens' minds. Even network executives are now admitting that media violence correlates with violence in viewers.

Fear   Many people do not see the connection between fear and anger, but this link is very real. People who have experienced severe or prolonged trauma fear being hurt again, much as a person with a broken arm fears being hit on that arm because even a small blow inflicts great pain. Fear is a normal response to the threat of rejection, failure, punishment, the unknown, exposure, and other potential sources of pain. Our instinctive response to these threats is anger at the person or thing that threatens us. In today's society, the threats are very real. Today's young people fear gang violence, date rape, pressure from dope-dealing friends, and sexually transmitted diseases. There's a lot to be afraid of . . . and angry about.

Unrealistic Expectations   Young people have unrealistic expectations. They may expect to make the honor roll even though they don't study. They may expect to be a starter on the football team even though someone else is a better athlete. They think parents should give them money and friends should give them approval even if their performance or behavior doesn't warrant these rewards.

Young people see college athletes sign multimillion-dollar contracts to play professional sports. They hear of people who win fortunes playing the lottery. Television commercials tell them that if they use a certain product they will be happy, popular, and comfortable. And when these high expectations aren't met, they feel cheated. They feel angry.

PEER PRESSURE

Peer pressure is often labeled the number-one cause of alcohol and drug abuse among young people, but it needs to be seen in context with other causes. Adolescents ask questions like "Who am I?" and "What am I going to do with my life?" and look to their peers for answers. These normal, healthy questions become much more difficult to answer, however, if the adolescent's sense of security is threatened by upheaval at home or unresolved pain. They are then much more vulnerable to pressure from friends to try alcohol, drugs, sex, vandalism, or a host of other ways to fit in with the group. Insecurity leaves them emotionally weak and incapable of risking rejection. "Come on. Just *try* it. It won't kill you!" peers cajole, and the emotionally needy adolescent's desire to be accepted makes him susceptible to this seemingly harmless first act.

Rich played football, but he enjoyed several sports and couldn't decide which one to pursue. In his freshman year, he decided to play golf. He did fairly well, but all his buddies were on the baseball team. By his sophomore year, Rich was drinking beer with these friends every weekend and in November, when the time came to choose a spring sport, his friends encouraged him to play baseball. "Come on, Rich," his friend Bill said. "You'd have a great time with us, and besides, you don't want to hang around all those golf nerds another year, do you?"

But Rich played golf again. By the second week of practice, he realized he'd made the wrong choice. He missed his buddies on the baseball team. The next two years, Rich played baseball with his beer-drinking pals, and their friendship took him farther down the road of drinking and drug use. By midseason of his junior year, Rich was smoking grass with them regularly. And by the end of his senior year, they were using speed to get up for games. The progression was slow but steady. Each new door was opened by the usual comments: "Hey, one time never hurt anybody." "Man, this is the best stuff anybody ever had. We're lucky to get it!" "Nobody will ever know."

The media accentuates this pressure by depicting drinking as the perfect way to have a good time with friends. The thousands of beer commercials adolescents see each year are becoming increasingly sophisticated and seductive. In *It's Killing Our Kids*, Jerry Johnston notes that the message of Michelob's commercials has slowly and subtly evolved over the years. In 1980, the slogan was "Weekends are made for Michelob," but that changed to "Put a little weekend in your week." Finally, the advertising geniuses came up with "The night belongs to Michelob." In only a few years, the message progressed from suggesting casual drinking on weekends to more aggressively promoting nightly drinking.[4]

PARENTAL MODELING

Authorities debate the existence of a genetic link in alcoholism and drug dependency. There is evidence to support both sides of the issue. But there is little debate about the powerful effects of parents on the choices teenagers make. Adults who hypocritically say "Do as I say, not as I do" give the message that it is okay to drink or use drugs, and it is okay to be hypocritical. These messages reinforce denial that the substances have any ill effects on individuals or families.

It is difficult to overestimate the impact of parents on the perceptions and behaviors of children in every area of life. Everything parents do has a powerful influence on the behavior of their sons and daughters.

Another parental characteristic that shapes children is being too strict or too permissive. Studies show that both extremes are harmful to the development of a child's identity and ability to make healthy choices. Strict parents shelter their children by imposing high expectations and harsh consequences that rob the child of love, strength, and confidence. Permissive parents let their children go, either out of ignorance that their children need guidance as well as love, or because they are too preoccupied with their own problems to give their children time and attention. The resulting physical and emotional isolation leaves the child with an undeveloped emotional and moral base. Consequently, he or she may have difficulty making decisions, become rigid in reaction to the permissiveness, or look for others to tell him or her what to do. Obviously, young people may try to soothe the emotional pain created by the imbalance of rigidity or permissiveness with alcohol or drugs. And "friends" are only too ready to lend a hand in helping them find relief. At that point, bad decisions are easy to make.

Alcohol is the most widely accepted drug in our culture, and it has devastating effects. Drunk driving is the leading cause of death for people under twenty. It rips families apart and shatters lives. And alarmingly, 25 percent of those who use alcohol combine it with some other drug.[5]

In recent years, the fall and rise of one of the NBA's brightest stars has demonstrated both the devastation of drugs and the possibility of hope and healing. John Lucas was the Houston Rockets' first pick in the 1976 draft. The star point guard out of the University of Maryland seemed destined to bring glory to himself and his new team. But ten years later, drugs had stolen that glory. One day in 1986, Lucas wandered filthy and barefoot on a downtown street, unable to find his car, unable to remember how he got there. He failed a drug test that day and sat out that night's game with Portland. Sportswriter Mickey Herskowitz of the *Houston Post* wrote at that time:

> The tragedy of John Lucas is this: There was nothing in his life—not his family, his profession, his teammates, his reputation, not even money—that he held so dear he could not give them up for the moment of pleasure he enjoyed from drugs. . . .
> If a bright, attractive, talented, savvy fellow like John Lucas can't figure it out, what does it take? Did any athlete ever hit Houston with a bigger future than the one we quickly dubbed "Cool Hand Luke"? He was no reject, no dropout, but the product of a stable home, the son of two educators, good enough at tennis to play

the game for a living. There was nothing to dislike about John Lucas.

In Lucas's book, *Winning a Day at a Time*, he chronicles his descent into the abyss of addiction and his struggle to find a purpose in life apart from drugs. His recovery is one of the great stories in sports, and today he is respected by coaches and players—not only for his sports abilities but for his character.

Lucas reflected on the turning point: "I don't like some of the things I did. I made some wrong choices. I had to accept a lot of pain that night in March 1986, sitting on that bench and knowing I had told one of the biggest lies of my life. But I was too afraid to ask for help. Bill Fitch saved my life."

Lucas's "biggest lie" was his repeated insistence that he was straight and sober. Rockets coach Bill Fitch saved his life by forcing him to take a drug test and admit his problem.

Recovery from his addiction was difficult and painful, and some of his fans made it even worse. When Lucas returned to the court, one man yelled, "Don't snort the foul line, Lucas!" In another city, a fan slapped John on the back. Lucas appreciated the encouragement, but the fan had something else in mind. The victim of a classic junior high prank, Lucas unknowingly walked on the court with a sign taped to his jersey that read, "Things go better with coke."

Over the past few years, Lucas has actively helped those who have drug problems. He started a drug treatment center in Houston, opened a halfway house, and coached a basketball team composed of former addicts. Today Lucas is a beacon of hope for athletes caught in the jaws of drug addiction.

Lucas traces the roots of his addiction to the unreality of being a sports celebrity. "As a young kid, I am Jennifer Capriati," he said. "I am very much Monica Seles. We never grow up. We are pushed and pampered as young athletes and move into an adult world overnight, as Andre Agassi talks about it. You get into this competitive mold, and you don't know when to shut it off. I got addicted because I was always competing."

But John Lucas has beaten his addiction, and he offers strength, encouragement, and an example of one man who refused to give up or give in to the devastating consequences of drug addiction.[6]

For more information about drug and alcohol abuse, contact the following.

- American Council for Drug Education, 204 Monroe Street, Rockville, Maryland 20850, 212-758-8060.
- Parents' Resource Institute for Drug Education (PRIDE), The Hurt Building, 50 Hurt Plaza, Suite 210, Atlanta, Georgia 30303, 404-577-4500.
- U.S. Clearinghouse, National Clearinghouse for Alcohol and Drug Information (NCADI), P.O. Box 2345, Rockville, Maryland 20852, 301-468-2600.

3

SAFE OR OUT AT HOME?

The home atmosphere for pro golfer Betsy King provided the example, wisdom, and strength she needed for her life. Betsy's parents gave her a good foundation.

Betsy King

Professional golfer on the LPGA tour

I have always avoided drugs and alcohol because I knew they could only hurt my athletic performance. Even before I was a Christian, I had strong feelings about drinking and drugs. I didn't want anything to prevent me from doing my best on the course.

One of the big factors in whether you drink is who you hang around. If you hang around a wild group of people, then drinking and drugs will be more of a temptation. I made some choices all along the way to spend time with people who cared about the things I cared about. Wild parties

just weren't attractive to me. Following Christ and athletic perform-
ance were—and are—important to me.

My parents were good examples to me. My coaches, especially
in high school, always had rules to avoid drinking or smoking. These
guidelines taught me that these things were bad for me, and the
players on our team felt the same way. None of us wanted to hurt
our performance, so we didn't even consider drinking or using drugs.
At the professional level, I can't imagine anyone performing out here
with an alcohol or drug problem. You may be able to make it for a
while, but it catches up to you and wrecks your career.

People who use drugs or alcohol aren't in control of their lives.
Obviously, it affects their ability to succeed. Sometimes young
people think they have to experience something in order to know if
it's right or wrong. You don't have to do that. You don't have to jump
off a cliff to be convinced that it will hurt you! It's the same with
drugs and alcohol. I've seen people who have been hurt by using
and drinking. I don't have to use it myself to know how it would
affect me. Don't make the mistake of thinking you have to try
something to know that it's not right for you.

I know some Christians disagree about whether it's okay for
believers to drink. Obviously the Scriptures say we shouldn't get
drunk, but they also say that we are to be obedient to the law of
the land. And it is against the law for teenagers to buy and drink
or do drugs. If that's the only reason for teenagers not to drink, I
believe they should obey the laws of our country, states, and
communities.

Athletics provide great opportunities for young people, but if you
want to perform well, you have to take care of your body. That
includes not abusing it with alcohol or drugs. I get to meet a lot of
successful people in this life, and there is a very, very, very small
percentage of those people who abuse their bodies and are still
successful.

Football legend Bart Starr comments on the consequences of

using alcohol and drugs. He then gives parents some encouragement and direction for helping their teenagers make good choices.

Bart Starr

Former All-Pro quarterback for the Green Bay Packers

Student athletes often don't realize the seriousness of drug and alcohol abuse. The consequences can be severe. In fact, it's one of the most difficult challenges young people face today. I know this all too well, because six years ago, our youngest son, Bret, died of a massive heart attack after five years of serious drug abuse. The pain of our loss will never go away for my wife and me.

Young people need to establish priorities centered around a strong faith in God. The family is the second greatest source of strength and wisdom. A strong relationship with God and their families gives young people a sense of responsibility. If they won't compromise these priorities, they can stay strong in the face of temptations and peer pressures.

Here's one way to look at drug and alcohol abuse: If you received a new Mustang, there is no way you would pour sand in the gas tank because you know it won't run with sand in it. In the same way, if you fill your body with drugs or alcohol, you won't be able to function. And you will pay a tremendous price for that mistake. Most young people have never thought of it quite that way, but this analogy makes a lot of sense to a lot of people.

I want to encourage young people to find sources of strength to turn to: If peers try to pressure you to drink or do drugs, use the buddy system. Go immediately to find a friend who is clean and straight who cares about you.

Parents need to look for signs in their children, and they need to respond to those signs. If their youngster's mood has changed dramatically, the circle of friends has changed, he's now late and inconsistent, and any other types of behavior which are different from the way he has been in the past, these are red flags for parents. When parents see these things, they need to move quickly to find out what is happening. Sit down and begin communicating with your son or daughter. This may be difficult, but parents need to force themselves to start communicating, and they need to really work at it. Of course, this communication comes much easier if the parents have developed a real friendship with their children over the years so that the children look to their parents as some of their best friends.

Our priorities make a tremendous difference in our relationships. If we make the mistake of putting ourselves first instead of God and then our families, we—and our families—will be in deep trouble. Mixed up priorities are creating a lot of the problems in our society and in our own families. We are too individualistic, selfish, egotistical, and self-centered. We don't function as a team or a family to encourage and help one another. But we can. We can take strong steps to change priorities, to center our lives on God and let our relationships, desires, and activities be shaped by Him.

Jill's mother had had enough. She couldn't—or wouldn't—take any more of Jill's problems at home or at school. "Go ahead and take those stupid pills," she screamed at Jill, "but they won't help you!" She stopped a second, then said in disgust, "I've had it with you, Jill!"

Drug and alcohol abuse doesn't occur in a vacuum. It is an attempt to escape pain, rejection, abandonment, and heartache in the closest relationships in our lives. When we say that drugs and alcohol are a family problem, we're not saying that everyone in the family drinks and uses. We're saying that the family dynamics which produce substance abuse typically follow a predictable pattern. There are many different varieties of this pattern, but the foundational elements are similar, including denial, mistrust, and manipulation.

DENIAL

The phone rang and Mrs. Turner awoke from a deep sleep. She glanced at the clock. It read 3:17 A.M. "Hello," she mumbled. "Yes, this is Mrs. Turner." After a few more seconds of listening to the voice on the other end of the line, her voice became more animated. "I . . . I think you must have made a mistake, officer. That couldn't be my son. He doesn't do things like that."

Sometimes parents face the truth of a child's substance abuse only after the police—or the coroner—break the news. Parents don't want to believe that their son or daughter could be making such a mess of his or her life, so they dismiss all the warning signs.

Friends, parents, and coaches sometimes minimize a young person's problems. "Yeah, I know his eyes have been bloodshot lately, " a coach said to his assistant. "He's probably been studying a lot. School is tough these days, Bill. That's his only problem—too much studying."

Or they might acknowledge a teenager's substance abuse, but say, "Well, boys will be boys!" They prefer to believe their son was just "having a beer every now and then." True, he drank beer when he was in junior high. But now he's doing speed and smoking crack. He's tried LSD a few times lately, and he liked it. He is also still drinking beer, and it has been a lot more often than "every now and then."

Instead of each person taking responsibility for his or her behavior, family members (and team members) excuse and blame. "Roger can't help the way he's acting at school," his mother told the principal. "His father left two years ago, and Roger doesn't have anybody to show him how a man should act." Instead of helping Roger deal with the reality of his anger and rebellion, his mother excuses him and blames his father for his problems.

MISTRUST

Even in the healthiest of environments, it is difficult to learn who and how much to trust. Some people seem trustworthy, but they aren't. Others seem very passive, but they come through when they're needed most. We discover whether people are trustworthy by seeing how they respond in all types of situations.

But the other half of the trust equation is us. Some of us blindly trust even the most untrustworthy people. We may be trying to swap our trust for love and safety, or we may want so much to feel safe that we close our eyes to the instability around us. Blindly trusting others is an attempt to get them to treat us the way we want to be treated, but it doesn't work.

On the other hand, some of us refuse to trust even those who have proven over and over again to be trustworthy. We may have been hurt so badly or so often that we have given up on those around us, and we withdraw into emotional and physical isolation. Others try to dominate and intimidate instead of quietly withdrawing. These people have to be on top and in charge. That way, they can control others around them through anger and demands and gain a sense of superiority.

Children are born with an instinctive trust of their parents and their environment. They need physical provisions of food, clothing, and shelter, but they also have profound emotional needs for attention, affection, and touch. In fact, meeting these emotional needs is critical to their development. After World War II, a study of war orphans showed that many of the infants who were fed but not held died from the absence of cuddling and emotional affirmation. Their basic bodily needs were met, but their emotional needs were not.[1]

Parents don't have to be perfect to provide a trustworthy environment for their children. They only have to be good enough to model love and encourage family members to communicate and resolve conflict in healthy ways. Healthy families generally have the following characteristics.

- They are open and honest about the reality of stress in life.
- They communicate feelings, desires, and commitments.
- They adapt to changes.
- They help each other resolve conflicts.
- They affirm and encourage each other.

In contrast, unhealthy families generally have these characteristics.

- They view stress as abnormal and to be avoided at all costs.
- They either repress their feelings or explode (or both).
- They are rigid in expectations of themselves and others.
- They blame each other for failures or mistakes.
- They control each other through anger, manipulation, withdrawal, non-verbals, etc.[2]

The paradox is that much of the behavior in unhealthy families is designed to *avoid* stress, but it *creates even more*. This cycle produces even more hurt, anger, and confusion, and it further energizes our desire to escape pain and earn approval. The more unresolved hurt and anger we have, the more our perceptions and capacity to trust will be distorted. Our relationships will be blocked, shallow, intense, unrealistic, and painful, and we will be more likely to try to prove ourselves or numb our pain any way we can. One statistic is indicative of families in which the children feel abandoned by parents who are too busy to care for them: "Children left at home alone for eleven hours or more each week are nearly twice as likely to use alcohol, tobacco, and marijuana as are children under adult supervision."[3]

MANIPULATION

"If you can't trust, you have to control," is a principle of life in many families and teams. Feelings of safety and security allow us to relax, to be ourselves, to let our defenses down. But if we feel unsafe, we will try to control others and limit their capacity to hurt us. It's only natural, and in cases where others are abusive and harmful, it is necessary. The problem comes when we don't have the perception to determine whom we can trust and how we can extend our trust in appropriate ways. A second problem is that when we are stuck in a rut, we respond to everyone the same way, simply because that's the pattern we've learned. Some of us try to control others by:

Pleasing Them at All Costs We change our behavior, our attitudes, and our feelings to make others happy. We look like humble servants when we act this way, but we are trying to manipulate others to get the love and acceptance we want.

Giving in To avoid conflict, we let others have their way. "Oh I don't care. Whatever you want to do," we may say. "You always know what the right decision is. You decide."

Getting away Another way to limit others' capacity to hurt us is to avoid them. Some of us go into solitude in our rooms. Some of us move across the country. Some of us simply hide behind a newspaper, magazine, or book, or become absorbed in television.

Dominating Instead of avoiding conflict, some of us create conflict to threaten others, keep them off balance, and dominate them. Some people distort the spirit of friendly competition and demand to win at all costs. Being "one up" on someone gives them power over the other, but it certainly doesn't build good relationships with the one who feel "one down."

ROLES IN THE FAMILY

Authorities who have studied families under stress have noted that each member plays a certain role to minimize stress and allow the family to function without addressing the real issues. Each is an attempt to gain some sense of significance and avoid problems, and each role is effective in its own way.

The Comic   The Comic tries to make stress go away by making jokes or being silly: *Whenever his mother blew up at his dad, Bob laughed and said something like, "Hey, Mom, it's not like Dad's Adolf Hitler or something. He doesn't even have a mustache!" Most of the time, his mother ignored him and continued her tirade, but occasionally—enough times to make him think his efforts at humor were worth it—she just shook her head and walked away. That averted the crisis. Bob's goal was accomplished.*

The Fixer   The Fixer funnels her energies into solving everybody else's problems: *After the divorce, Janice's mother was depressed and withdrawn, so Janice took over many of her mother's responsibilities. Two years later, she was still the surrogate mom to her brother and sisters. Her mother's powerful combination of self-pity and affirmation—"I don't know what I'd do without you!"—fueled Janice's behavior. She felt needed, but the pattern of her mother's irresponsibility and Janice's assumption of responsibility had become fixed and permanent.*

The Hero   The Hero finds a way to be somebody by excelling in sports, school, work, or some other endeavor: *Gerald's family moved every year or so. His relationships were shallow because it hurt too much to get close and then be pulled apart again. And the stress level in the family was high. Gerald desperately wanted to be accepted, and he had some basketball skills. He was driven to excel so he could be somebody.*

The Mole   The Mole hides from stress physically and emotionally and limits others' access so they can't hurt her again: *Sherry had an escape hatch—the stairs. She functioned normally as a member of the family, helping with cooking and cleaning and taking her brother to school and practice—until her parents began yelling at each other. When that happened, she immediately exited upstairs to her room. She shut the door, turned on her CD player, and put on her headphones, trying to lose herself in the music and forget the tense, hateful scene downstairs.*

The Nice Person   The Nice Person hides his or her anger behind a mask of kindness, pleasantness, and positiveness: *"Sandy's such a sweet girl!" everybody said. "I've never heard Sandy utter an unkind word about anybody," her teacher told her parents. But Sandy was unnaturally sweet. She wouldn't let herself feel pain and anger. Her way to cope with her fear of rejection was to be so sweet, kind, and thoughtful that nobody would ever be upset with her. She had lots of superficial friends; she was afraid of letting anybody know her hidden thoughts. So she felt very lonely. The wall of niceness that blocked others' rejection also kept out their love.*

The Slicer   The Slicer cuts people to ribbons with vicious sarcasm, and when confronted says in surprise, "Hey, I was only kidding!": *Everybody laughed at Jimmy. His quick wit and funny one-liners made him popular with his buddies, but they all stayed on their toes because they'd seen him cut people down with biting, "humorous" comments. His targets felt hurt, but almost no one said anything because he would deny he meant any harm, and they would lose their place in his circle of friends if they were too sensitive.*

The Commander   The Commander has to be in charge of every person and every situation: *Ken was a born leader. When he walked in the room, everybody knew he would be the focus of attention and the decision-maker. Sometimes he was charming, but if someone had the nerve to disagree with him, Ken could be brutal, questioning their intelligence or integrity. Somehow he always dominated the group.*

The Scapegoat   The Scapegoat takes the blame for all the family's problems: *Donna's father lost his job—again. Her mother had been fed up with him for years and found excitement in the arms of other men. Donna's two brothers dropped off the football team just before they were kicked off for all kinds of behavior problems. And they all blamed Donna. She overheard her father tell a friend, "If Donna didn't always whine about having more, I wouldn't feel so much pressure and mess up at work!" Her mother told her, "I just can't count* on you at all! Your father tries so hard, but you're a flake!" And her brothers told their friends, "Donna won't help Mom enough around the house. Then Mom gets so mad that it really messes up the whole family. We've got to quit football and get jobs because Dad's so stressed out over Donna that he can't keep a job." And Donna believes them.

The Volcano The Volcano is dormant until the pressure builds, then he erupts in violent rage: *Phil had seen it before. His dad would remain placid until something pushed him over the edge. Then he'd clench his teeth, curse, and throw whatever was in reach. He might go for days or even weeks without losing control, but sooner or later, the top came off. Everybody was too afraid of him to say anything about his rage.*

The Doctor All of these responses to hurt and anger work for a while, but eventually they fail to block the pain. Then the person may become The Doctor, who medicates the patient by prescribing the drug of choice: alcohol, amphetamines, food, sex, or something else.[4]

Of course, people can play more than one role at a time, and they sometimes change roles if a trauma (such as death, disease, divorce, relocation, or any major loss or disruption) tilts the balance of needs in the family.

Many of the people who play these roles don't *appear* hurt or angry. That's the point. They don't want people to know the depth of their pain because that information would make them vulnerable. Their goals are to hide their emotions, to get revenge by hurting others aggressively or passively, to find some sense of meaning in life, and to control their environments. The different roles focus on one or more of these goals.

All the roles we've described are attempts to deal with confusion, despair, and heartache without bringing the causes out into the open for examination, discussion, and resolution. A person using speed may or may not be more angry and hurt than an athlete who is passionate about being All-District and becomes deeply depressed when he doesn't make it. His addiction, however, is less socially acceptable. Drive and determination in athletics is a good trait—unless it is just another way to escape the pain.

"IT'S NEVER ENOUGH"

Even in the best families, people experience a fair share of hurt and anger. In emotionally healthy families, people are encouraged to talk openly about their problems and resolve them through compromise, understanding, and forgiveness. In unhealthy families, however, the unresolved hurt and anger festers and multiplies, eroding trust, communication, and love. Self-confidence becomes hopelessness. "No matter what I do, it's not enough," is too often the response of those who have heard, "You're a failure. You've always been a failure, and you'll always be one!"

But sometimes this message is communicated in very different words. The message, "You can't do enough," comes across loud and clear in the statement, "I'm counting on you to win the championship. You've got to do it!" Those words inspire, but they also carry an implied threat. Coaches, parents, and friends need to examine the underlying message and implications of this kind of "encouragement." Sometimes our words produce zeal based on fear instead of a desire to excel.

Over time, fear and shame produce a victim mentality. This perspective recognizes the hard knocks we've had, the injustices we've experienced, and the pain we've endured and demands that somebody fix these injustices by making us happy, successful, and popular. Victims demand that someone—a parent, a spouse, a coach, a friend, or someone else—protect them from these injustices. Their self-pity makes them easily offended and prickly as a porcupine. When people get near a victim, they're often pricked by the victim's defensiveness and demands, so they learn not to get too close.

Victims want some kind of guarantee of protection that people won't mistreat them again. But in the real world with real people, bumps and bruises are inevitable. When we react to the normal problems of life with more than normal anger, it reveals our deeper, unresolved wounds.

LOOK AT THE FAMILY SYSTEM

A friend who is a Christian counselor said:

Adolescents (and adults, too, for that matter) don't abuse alcohol or drugs in a vacuum. But young people who abuse alcohol and drugs don't get better in a vacuum either. The dynamics in the family are almost always a big contributing factor. If the teenager wants to change but her parents and siblings continue to deny or minimize the problem, it will be tremendously difficult for her to make progress. Ideally, everybody in the family will see the manipulation, the roles they've played, and they all will seek help. But the ideal is seldom reality. If *only one* other person in the family will be honest and seek help, that increases the likelihood of progress quite a lot! So, if nobody else in the family wants help, have the courage to get it anyway.

Drinking or using is not the main problem. Alcohol and drugs are only ways—just like school, sex, work, and food—to escape the pain of rejection, failure, fear, and loneliness. Both the behavior and the underlying cause of that behavior need to be identified and addressed before there can be long-term, substantive change.

A person's home environment is the single most important factor in shaping his ability to respond positively to temptations. Sometimes, this ability is tested in junior high school, often in high school, and sometimes even beyond school. Darrell Porter, star catcher for the Royals and Cardinals, found the stresses and loneliness of professional baseball too much to take.

Darrell Porter

Former catcher for the Kansas City Royals and St. Louis
Cardinals; World Series MVP in 1982

*I started drinking when I left home
after I graduated from high school. I was
beginning my career in professional
baseball. I never took a drink in high
school because I didn't think athletes
were supposed to. I thought it would
hurt your athletic performance, and athletics were my whole life. But when I left
home, sports became much more difficult because I was playing against people who were professionals. Most of*
them had been playing longer, so they were better than me. That
was really hard. I had never struggled in sports before.*

*There's an old adage in baseball: "When you're struggling, go have
a beer! Relax and forget it!" Some guys on the team kept inviting me
to go out with them for a beer. I put them off for a while, but then
the hurt of being away from home, being lonely, not doing well in
baseball, and not having any other friends—all that got to me, and
I decided to go with them. We were in Appleton, Wisconsin, and
we went to this little bar with pool tables and a dance floor. We sat
at a table, and one of my buddies said, "We're going to drink until
we fill this table up with beer bottles!" I just wanted to fit in, so I
joined them. I felt pretty lonely. I didn't really have anybody but
these guys, no family, no friends. I remember crying at night because
I was so lonely. These guys wanted me to be one of their buddies.
This was a chance to fit in.*

*I remember telling them when I drank that first beer, "Man, this
tastes bad!" And they told me, "Don't worry. The next one won't
taste so bad." And it didn't. After about four beers, I could have cared
less that I was hitting .182 and I was alone, without my family or
friends! I learned that very night that I'd discovered something that*

would make me feel better. Beer was a new friend that I could call on when times were tough, and it would make me feel better.

The next winter, I went home, and my buddies at home were doing marijuana. Believe it or not, I had never even heard of marijuana! They asked me to try it, and it was really easy to say yes because I had stepped over the line once to drink beer. Stepping over again was easy. Smoking marijuana made me feel really good! I couldn't believe how much I laughed! I really enjoyed smoking it. Some time after that, I started using downers, and later, cocaine. I was feeling really down and out after the 1979 season. That year, I decided to really concentrate on being the best player I could be. I thought if I could do well, I would feel really good about myself. That year, I had my best season. In fact, only one catcher has ever had a better season than I had that year. But when the season was over, I realized that nothing had changed. I still had a big hole in me. I could walk down any street in America, and people would say, "Hey, Darrell, you're the best catcher in baseball!" I had a pretty girl, a big house, nice cars, money, and everything, but I still felt as empty as before. I thought, "Good night! What I thought was going to satisfy me didn't at all." I became deeply depressed and escalated my drug use dramatically. I was using three or four grams of cocaine a day.

By the time the next spring training rolled around, I had given up on myself and baseball. God sent a man named Don Newcombe, who used to pitch for the Dodgers, to speak to our team. Don had been an alcoholic, and drinking had destroyed his career. The league sent him around to speak to the players to help anybody who had a problem. The Lord sent him for me. He asked us some questions about alcohol and drug use, and he said if you answered any three of them yes, you have a problem. I answered all of them yes! I thought that maybe if I quit drugs, I could get my life back together.

I went out to the field and asked one of my buddies, "Would you go in and tell Don Newcombe I need talk to him because I have a problem?" And he said, "Man, you don't have any problem!" He didn't want me to admit I had a problem because then he might have to admit he had a problem too. But I asked him again, and Don helped me get into a treatment program.

Before I left, a player on our team, Jerry Terrell, came to me and said, "Come on, friend. I want you to go with me." Jerry took me with him to buy me a Bible. I went to the treatment program and began to read that Bible. Right after I got there, I found a passage of Scripture, Jeremiah 29:13: "And you will seek Me and find Me, when you search for Me with all your heart." I'd always wondered if there was a God, but this verse became my hope. I said, "I'm going to search for God with all my heart and find out if God is real."

About five years later, after constantly studying the Bible and fellowshiping with good believers, God worked in my heart. I went to the Cardinals, and there were some really strong Christians on that team. I spent time with them going to chapel, praying, and talking. In a hotel room, one night in New York City in 1985, I looked out the window and saw people partying and drinking in the streets. I sat on my bed and started praying, and it was like the ceiling of my room opened up, and I was engulfed in the presence of God. For the first time in my life, I knew God was with me. At that moment, there was no doubt in my mind that God was there and that Jesus Christ was who the Bible said He was. In that moment, I was changed. That was when I trusted Christ as my Savior.

I sure wish I hadn't used drugs because I lost my relationship with my family and friends. Drugs made me so selfish. I just didn't care about them anymore. I only cared about me and getting more drugs. I lost these relationships. That hurts really bad even as I think about it now. Also, I know . . . I know drugs destroyed my baseball career. People look at my successes, and they might have a hard time understanding that statement, but God gave me a lot of baseball talent. I blew it. My career would have been longer and better if I hadn't messed it up with drugs.

I want to encourage young people: Take it from me. I've been there. Drugs are—no question—a one-way street to hell. There is no way you can survive using drugs and alcohol. They will destroy your life. Don't even start. The very first time I did it, I was hooked. There's no guarantee that you won't be like me, hooked from the first drink.

4

BLACK BEAUTY AIN'T A HORSE!

Dal Shealy

President of The Fellowship of Christian Athletes;
former head coach of the Richmond University Spiders

Several years ago, one of our offensive linemen was engaged to a local girl who lived in a neighboring community. Just before two-a-days began, he went to see her. During this visit, his fiancée's mother angrily gave her daughter's engagement ring back to him. She told him not to ever come back.

On the first day of practice, this young man had a fever, so the doctor put him on medication. The trainers took meals to his dorm room to take care of him and check on him. While we were at practice the second day, he left the dorm and and drove to a large discount store. That night, he came to our team meeting. He was smiling and talking with the guys. He seemed to be feeling better.

But sometime in the middle of the night, he slipped out of the dorm past the coaches who were staying there. He bought some beer, and his medication accentuated the effects of the alcohol.

He drove out to his ex-fiancée's house and got in. The girl's brother woke up, and the two of them got in a fight. The football player grabbed a hunting knife and stabbed the brother, who ran to a neighbor's house.

The mother heard the commotion and came to the top of the stairs. When she turned on the light, the young man's hatred seethed in him. He took out the gun he had bought that afternoon at the store and blasted her with two shots. He then went upstairs to the girl's room. He grabbed her and took her into the bathroom. Just like Romeo and Juliet, he shot her because he couldn't live without her. He wanted to live in eternity with her, so he put the gun to his right eye and blew the back of his head off.

I got a phone call at five o'clock in the morning. The campus police asked me to come to the station. I expected to find one of our players who had been caught speeding or drinking. Those are the types of problems I usually face. Instead, the campus policeman drove me to a house with yellow tape all around it. You can imagine the scene as we went up the stairs and tried to identify the bodies. Alcohol, medication, and the broken engagement proved to be a lethal and tragic combination.

That same year we had a starting quarterback who was a great athlete, an All-State performer in high school. He could execute as well as anyone, but if he took a big hit, on the next play he got nervous. He would fumble the snap, hurry a pass, throw an interception, and blow the play.

One Sunday morning after a game in which he got hit very hard, he told the trainer he had a problem: blood in his urine. The doctors ran tests, but they couldn't find any significant cause of the problem. They told him that it probably came from a hit he took in the game.

The next Saturday, he made a great run down to the one yard line, and he got plastered! The next play, he fumbled the snap. The ball went into the end zone and the other team recovered for a touchback. The next day, he went to the trainer with the same problem: blood in his urine.

The doctors put him in the hospital for a couple of days, but they couldn't find a conclusive answer to the problem. This pattern of bleeding after games went on for three or four weeks. Our trainer then spoke with a sports doctor who said that it was possible that these symptoms could be the result of drinking alcohol and smoking marijuana.

The trainer told me what the doctor said, and on the following Monday, I took the young man aside after the quarterback meeting. I looked him in the eye and asked him, "How long have you been smoking marijuana and drinking beer?"

His eyes got as big as saucers. He asked how I knew, and I told him what the doctor suspected about the cause of blood in his urine. I told him his behavior was costing his team some ballgames. I asked him if he could stop smoking dope and drinking. He replied that he might be able to stop drinking, but he didn't know if he could stop smoking dope.

I asked him to bring his dad in to see me the next day. I explained to his father that I was going to keep his son on scholarship so he could finish his degree, but since he wouldn't stop smoking, I was going to have to dismiss him from the team.

This young man graduated and went on to work in a bank. I hope and pray that his life is heading in the right direction. He could have been a truly outstanding football player—maybe even a pro—if he had made better choices about drinking and smoking marijuana.

Skip and Patrick had been friends for years. They had been in the same class since the second grade. They were in the same Cub Scout pack and Boy Scout troop, and they played all kinds of sports together. When they were twelve, they went camping with some buddies in the Ozarks. On their way back to camp one afternoon, they walked through another campsite. It was deserted, but there were coolers next to a tent. The boys looked inside and found several six-packs of beer.

"Man, look at all this beer!" Skip said excitedly.

"Don't even think about it, Skip," a friend warned.

"Shoot, nobody is anywhere close," Skip waved off the skeptic. "And besides, they'll never miss a couple of brews."

Skip saw that a couple of his friends were hesitant about his plan to swipe the beer, but before he could say anything, Patrick told them, "Hey, if you want to drink some beer, stay. If you don't, then leave. I don't want to stand here all day jawing with you guys!"

All of the others left. Patrick and Skip licked their lips and grabbed a cold can of beer. "Man, this'll be great!" Skip said with a grin.

Drinking stolen beer that hot July day made the two boys feel powerful and grown-up. After that, they looked for new opportunities to drink, like the time a friend's parents were out of town for the weekend and had lots of beer in the basement refrigerator.

At first, their beer-drinking was exciting but infrequent. Then they found stores that didn't ask for ID. Beer-drinking became more frequent . . . and less stimulating. The thrill had worn off. So the boys tried malt liquor and some wine. They bought a gallon of cheap peach wine, but they hated it! Back to beer.

By the time they were sophomores, drinking had become an indispensable part of the weekend. They played varsity football, and they relaxed after the game with a few cool ones. On one occasion, they didn't have enough money for beer. They looked through both their houses, but all they could find was a large bottle of mouthwash. "Pat, you're not gonna drink that stuff are you?" Skip asked with a grimace.

"Hey, this stuff is fifty proof! It'll do the trick," Patrick assured him.

The boys rode around town that night chugging mouthwash until they got high. "I bet we got the freshest breath in town!" they joked.

That year, the boys went to a party where college students were serving mixed drinks. "Hey, where's the brew?" Patrick asked.

"That's for kids," a coed said with an all-knowing smile. "This is a lot better. What'll you have?"

"Whatever you've got!" Patrick said, trying to assure her that they weren't just kids.

The boys liked hanging around college students, and soon they *acquired a taste for liquor. A few months later, they noticed some of their new friends smoking marijuana. "Hey, Patrick, my man," one called to him. "Come here and try this weed. You'll like it."*

Patrick had smelled marijuana a hundred times before, and some of his friends smoked, but this was his first hit. He liked it. Skip tried it, too, but he wasn't as enthusiastic about their new find. Patrick enjoyed smoking with his new friends, and he spent as much time as possible with them. He began to neglect his studies. He even lost his motivation for football. His relationship with Skip showed some strain. "You've got to stop smoking that stuff, Patrick," Skip said. "It's messing with your mind!"

Patrick rolled his eyes and said sarcastically, "Okay, Mom! What time do you want me home from school, Mom?"

"Hey, man, I'm not your mom, and I'm not your friend much anymore either since you've been spending all your time with those potheads. Look at your life!" He paused. "And look at us." He paused again, then said sadly, "What happened to all the good times we used to have?"

"They're gone!" Patrick snapped. "That's what's happened to them! They're gone, and life goes on." The two old friends parted. The next time Skip saw him, Patrick had lost twenty pounds and was wearing a long-sleeved shirt in August to hide the needle marks in his arms.

As in Patrick's case, there is often a pattern of progression in the type of substance used:

1. entry-level beverages such as wine coolers and beer
2. cigarette smoking; liquor
3. marijuana
4. hard drugs[1]

For each of these stages, the pattern includes experimentation, regular use, and subsequently diminishing effects, which leads to experimentation with the next level of substances. Those who use hard drugs have almost certainly followed this progression. Patrick did follow that pattern.

Alcohol is the substance of choice for both adults and adolescents. In his book *Helping the Struggling Adolescent*, Les Parrott III, Ph.D., comments:

> Statistics vary but the best estimates indicate that there could be more than four million American alcoholics under the age of eighteen. And the age of experimentation is getting younger. Today's junior highers are facing decisions about drugs that were once reserved only for older youth. Trying alcohol today is already more common among current fifth graders than it was among current eighth graders when they were in the fifth grade. The percentage of youth who drank alcohol ten or more times in the last twelve months doubles between the eighth and ninth grades. Substance use among adolescents is a problem the size of Goliath. Each weekend 30 to 40 percent of the youth in America use alcohol and drugs.[2]

The motivations of teenagers to drink vary. Of the estimated ten million who drink, 25 percent drink to get high or because they are bored, 41 percent drink when they are upset, and 31 percent drink alone. These numbers are even higher for binge drinkers.[3]

But alcohol is not the only drug students use. Different researchers draw similar and alarming conclusions about the broad use of drugs. They find that by the time seniors graduate from high school:

- 93 percent have drunk alcohol
- 27 percent have used stimulants
- 16 percent have used cocaine
- 15 percent have used hallucinogens
- 14 percent have used barbiturates or sedatives
- 14 percent have used inhalants
- 13 percent have used tranquilizers
- 10 percent have used opiates
- 9 percent have used LSD
- 25 percent smoke marijuana regularly
- 33 percent get drunk at least once a month[4]

It is also notable that 34.4 percent of AIDS cases reported to the

Centers for Disease Control in 1992 were caused by intravenous drug use.[5]

ENTRY POINTS

The entry point for many young people is a relatively new product: wine coolers. These taste much like the fruit drinks children enjoy in their homes, so teens don't have to force themselves to drink something they don't like. Wine coolers are the beverage of choice for first-time drinkers, women, and children ten to thirteen.

Inhalants have become another favorite of younger people. When inhaled, fumes from household products such as glue, nail polish remover, paint thinner, and hairspray give users an almost instant high. But users develop tolerance quickly, needing more and more sniffs to get the same feeling. This paves the way to the use of more powerful drugs, though many who progress to other drugs continue to use inhalants too. The abuse of inhalants is even greater among teens than cocaine abuse. In 1992, 775,000 reportedly abused inhalants; 745,000 abused cocaine.[6]

Smokeless tobacco is yet another entry point for young people, and the statistics for this substance are alarming. The American Council for Drug Education reports that "one of three smokeless tobacco users began using as young as five years old, and the average age of first use is nine years. Nearly one in four white high school males uses spit tobacco."[7]

CIGARETTES

The tobacco industry has issued repeated denials of the addictive nature of cigarettes, but independent studies (and even secret tobacco industry studies) reveal that nicotine is highly addictive. And cigarette smokers are much more likely to experiment with other drugs and to become addicted to them as well. Former White House drug czar Robert L. Dupont Jr. learned that young cigarette smokers:

- use alcohol twice as much as nonsmokers
- use depressants and stimulants nine times more often
- smoke marijuana ten times more often
- are fourteen times more likely to use heroin, hallucinogens, or cocaine[8]

MARIJUANA

In a 1993–1994 study of 200,000 students in grades six through twelve in thirty-four states, the national Parents' Resource Institution for Drug Education (PRIDE) found a marked increase in marijuana use over the previous year. Among high school students, monthly use climbed from 11.3 percent to 15.6 percent, and the figures for junior high students rose from 3.3 percent to 4.9 percent. Lee Brown, current director of the White House Office of National Drug Control Policy, states, "Many of our young people no longer believe drug use is harmful. Or if they know the facts . . . [they] just don't care." Increased marijuana use is alarming, Brown said, because marijuana is at least ten times more potent than it was only ten years ago.[9]

Marijuana is the springboard to hard drugs. Once thought to be relatively harmless, marijuana is now known to have several harmful effects on users, including loss of motivation, reduced motor skills, reduced attention span, changes in personality, and mood swings. Those who use it regularly usually lose interest in everybody and everything except getting high. They also develop a tolerance to the drug and smoke more to get high. Today, there are strong types of marijuana available, and smokers eventually develop a tolerance to these strains too. Two-thirds then graduate to hard drugs to get the same sensation or to experience a different type of high.[10]

THE HARD STUFF

The culture of hard drugs is intensely self-focused. When a user gets to this stage, he is preoccupied with getting high as often as possible. He uses secrecy to hide his habit and is desperate for money to fund it. The spiral of dependence and secrecy draws him deeper and deeper into the abyss of isolation, hopelessness, and addiction. Money becomes a consuming drive. Authorities estimate that three out of five cocaine users become dealers to generate income. They then create their own market by enticing other students to try drugs. The kids try it, like it, become good customers, need more money, become dealers, and the pattern continues to expand.

There are four major types of drugs, and each affects the user in specific ways. Legitimate, legal, prescription drugs are found in each of these categories, and in fact, the abuse of prescription drugs is one of the most significant problems of substance abuse in America. The four major types of drugs include the following.

STIMULANTS

Stimulants heighten awareness and energy and decrease appetite. They can be useful in treating depression. Examples include caffeine, nicotine, diet pills (such as dextroamphetamine sulfate), speed, and cocaine.

DEPRESSANTS

Depressants slow down the nervous system and come in many varieties, including alcohol, minor tranquilizers (such as Valium), and sedatives. Other substances that can be used as depressants are glue, nail polish remover, cleaning fluid, gasoline, lighter fluid, and antifreeze.

NARCOTICS

Narcotics are powerful and highly addictive substances that relieve physical pain and produce a sense of euphoria. Examples include heroin, morphine, and codeine.

HALLUCINOGENS

Hallucinogens are illegal, "mind-expanding" drugs that have no helpful or medicinal use and include LSD, marijuana, and mescaline.[11]

STEROIDS

Steroids have also been abused by teens. Anabolic steroids stimulate the effects of testosterone, the male sex hormone, resulting in increasing muscle development, body hair, and bone size. The risks of using this drug include emotional and physical problems. Many users experience mood swings, "steroid rages," and depression. Many also develop acne, liver disease, and heart disease. Studies of teenage steroid use reveals that:

- 7 percent of male high school students have tried anabolic steroids
- 20 percent of high school athletes use steroids regularly
- teen steroid users are three times more likely to drink alcohol regularly
- steroid users are three times more likely to use marijuana and cocaine[12]

Athletes who succumb to the pressure to be stronger and bigger sometimes use this banned drug. In international competition, athletes from several countries have been suspected of using steroids to enhance their competitive edge. Female athletes using steroids often experience a dramatically changed appearance and develop muscle definition like men. In the United States, professional and college athletes have admitted taking steroids in recent years. Lyle Alzado's recent confession to steroid use and subsequent untimely death caused many to realize the dangers of this drug. Professional wrestler Hulk Hogan also admitted using steroids to build muscle mass.[13]

Coach Landry

Years ago, the league changed the rules so that it became an asset to be a big offensive lineman. When they changed the rules to put more offense into the game, they made it acceptable for offensive linemen to extend their arms when they were pass blocking. The coaches realized that their linemen needed to be bigger so they could use their hands and push defensive players off. Bigger players then had a great advantage, and steroids helped them put on a lot of weight very quickly. When a lineman weighs 270, 280, or 290, the defensive man just can't get around him. It is only relatively recently in the National Football League that they outlawed steroids.

People fifty and over have difficulty comprehending the variety and availability of drugs for youth today. Those of us from the Woodstock Age knew that marijuana was easy to find. We followed the example of role models like Jimi Hendrix and Dr. Timothy Leary, who encouraged us to experiment with anything and everything. But drugs are more accessible today than ever before, and some of the most addictive types, like crack, can be purchased by any seventh grader before, after, or even during a break at school. New drugs hit the streets every time some basement chemist produces a new type. Ice and XTC (pronounced "ecstacy") are perhaps the best known of the past few years, although the trend on the streets seems to be moving away from new, exotic drugs. Many users realize the inherent dangers in these untested substances. Instead, the street market is producing more powerful versions of marijuana and other common drugs. In addition, alcohol is growing even more in popularity. We can't pretend the danger isn't there. We need to be aware so we can educate and encourage these young people to make good choices. And we need to open ourselves to the sights and sounds of those who have made the wrong choices.

Miles McPherson

Former defensive back for the San Diego Chargers;
presently an evangelist

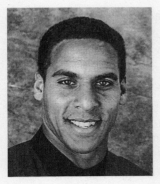

From the time I was sixteen until I was twenty-four, I smoked marijuana regularly. I also drank, and I used cocaine the last year and a half. I started purely out of curiosity. My friends were using it. I'm a high energy, "go-go," Type-A personality, and I always want to have as much fun and excitement as possible. My friends seemed to be having a good time, and I wanted to see what it was all about. I smoked about ten times before I ever got high, and after that, I smoked very regularly. I got accustomed to being "up," so I kept using it. I always vowed I could stop at any time, but I didn't stop. I didn't want to.

I didn't think using drugs affected my athletic performance at all until I got to the NFL. At that point, a couple of police officers told me that they could tell I was using drugs by the way I played. Whether they could tell by my play or not, they saw me spending time with other guys who were using drugs—some guys they had busted before. So they at least suspected I was using because of the people I hung around.

I never played high or practiced high. I always smoked or drank after practice or games. But drugs deceived me. I didn't want to believe that they affected my performance on the field, but they did. Using drugs made me believe that I didn't have to work as hard as I really needed to. I had a warped perception of how good I was. When you do drugs, you become numb to your responsibilities. You lose touch with reality, and therefore, you do things that aren't realistic. You assume things are going to be okay because you feel okay, but after a while, you find yourself in trouble, your athletic ability tapers off, and your attitude gets bad too. You may not think it affects you, but that's denial. It really affects you in a lot of different ways, both directly and indirectly. Some of my friends that I got high with got arrested. That affected their careers because they were then marked as drug users.

If I hadn't used drugs, I would have reached a level of excellence in football that I did not reach. I'll never know how much drugs hurt my performance, but I'm absolutely sure I never attained the level of excellence I could have attained because of drugs.

I walked into a hotel room when I was with the Chargers, and some guys on the team had some cocaine on the table. I was new to the team, and I wanted to fit in. Actually, I promised myself I would never touch that stuff, but that day, I wanted to fit in with my new teammates, so I tried it. I had no idea these guys had coke in the hotel room, but one of them said, "Hey, why don't you take a hit?" They had an "eight ball" (three and a half grams) of coke on the table. It was about three hundred dollars worth. They had the lines drawn and cut with a razor blade. Everyone else was doing it, and I figured I would just do it to fit in.

The minute I walked out of that room, I felt paranoid that everybody in the hotel knew that I had done cocaine! I kept looking over my shoulder thinking everyone knew I was high. But soon, I tried it again, and I really enjoyed it. It was a different kind of high than marijuana or alcohol. And at that point, I used cocaine regularly. It was my drug of choice. Guys on the team introduced me to their dealers, and pretty soon, I started making my own connections with dealers. I got my own phone numbers and my own connections in the drug culture so I could buy it.

Doing drugs ruined my relationship with the person I was dating because drugs were more important to me than being with her. Getting high with my friends was more important than being a faithful and consistent boyfriend. She felt slighted, like she was put in the back seat—which she was.

In my heart, I knew that if and when I would give my heart to Jesus, I would stop doing drugs and marry her. But I didn't want that to happen too soon because I wanted to party. I was having too much fun to stop.

There were nights I would lie on my bed, and my heart would almost pound through my chest. Literally, I was pretty close to a heart attack. When cocaine gets in your bloodstream, it dilates the blood vessels, and your heart races! Your heart goes into overdrive. That's how some athletes have died from cocaine. Don Rogers died that way. His heart just exploded! My heart would pound so much that I would be up twenty-four or thirty-six hours. My body got fatigued. I was in really good shape, so that compensated for the destruction somewhat, but doing drugs drained my body and hurt my performance.

Drugs distorted my focus and made me physically weaker than I could have been. I didn't actually feel weak, but I could have been stronger and healthier. I was always one notch lower than I could have been, but I got accustomed to that and thought it was normal. If I hadn't used drugs all those years, I would have been more dedicated in my diet, discipline, reading, workouts, and studies. I would have been one step more dedicated, more intelligent, and in shape. But I thought what I was experiencing was normal until I looked at guys with less ability than I had who were doing better than me because they weren't on drugs. It was frustrating. I knew I was a better athlete and just as intelligent as they were, but I didn't maximize my potential.

Some guys on my team who were Christians, Sherman Smith and Ray Preston, had a Bible study on a plane trip. They confronted me and shared the truth with me. These were guys I watched in the locker room. They had strength and purpose. I knew I needed what they had. One day at about five o'clock in the morning, I was lying on my couch. I had been up all night doing cocaine. Right then I decided I was through doing cocaine. I knew I needed to get my life together, get straightened out, and get married. At five o'clock in the morning, I said, "Lord, I'm giving my life to you right now. I'm going to be committed from this point forward." From that moment, I never got high again.

When I became a Christian, I was very committed to Christ. He was now what I depended on instead of drugs. He totally healed me and made me a new creature. I didn't have any withdrawal symptoms. That doesn't happen too often, but it happened to me.

Not long after I became a Christian, a friend of mine on the football team had some cocaine one night. He asked me if I wanted some, and I said no. When I said that, I felt a peace come over me. I felt the Lord was pleased with me. About a half hour later, he asked me again, and again I said no. This time the sense of peace came over me even stronger. I liked that so much that I followed him around so he would keep asking me so I could keep saying no and keep feeling stronger and more peaceful! Finally, he got mad at me because I wouldn't do cocaine with him. I looked at him, and I knew that my drug life was over. I said to myself, "The Lord is better, and I'm going to stick with Him." I passed those testing times, and God really blessed me with a peace that the drugs could never give me. Soon I started sharing my testimony about Christ, and God started showing me what he wanted me to do with my life.

I wish I had never started using drugs because it wasted eight years of my life.

5

KNOW THE SIGNALS

Peggy is the wife of Gary Cuozzo, former NFL quarterback for the Minnesota Vikings. Their son, Chip, was a star high school quarterback, but he became involved with drugs and was murdered in a drug deal in Miami on July 9, 1990.

Peggy Cuozzo

When I was pregnant with Chip, my daughter had German measles. Our doctor asked us to consider aborting our baby, but we never considered that option. Instead, we prayed, and our friends prayed. A few months later, Chip was born—a very healthy little boy. I knew he was a special gift from God.

Chip was very bright, very athletic, but very shy. As I look back now, I think that was a major part of the problem. Even as a young child, he was afraid to try because he was afraid to fail. When he had the courage to try, he excelled. When he was in the eighth grade, he was chosen as a Pop Warner Scholar Athlete. There were only thirty in the country. Chip was harassed by his classmates who said things on the playground like, "Let's see what you can do!" That was really hard on Chip, and it made him even more shy.

When Chip started high school, he had to get a physical to play football. The doctor asked him, "Are you going to play pro ball?" This kind of expectation put a lot of pressure on a young boy. The pressure increased because Chip was such a star athlete and the other kids made fun of him for getting so much attention. And beyond that, he was in the honors program in academics, so the kids harassed him for that too. Chip began to fall apart, and he developed discipline problems.

When he was a senior, Chip was a star quarterback. He was the homecoming king, but he was so shy he didn't want to go to the dance. His friends had to come get him so he would go. But nobody would ever know he was so shy. He had all the "costumes" of being cool—the clothes, the talk, the look—and he hung around the cool group.

During his senior year, Chip thought he needed to gain some weight to be prepared for college ball. He started taking steroids and lifting weights, and in only a few months, he gained from 190 to 220 pounds. During this time, he developed a "steroid rage," and his anger caused him to be the center of attention for the family.

He got a scholarship to Holy Cross, but by the end of his freshman year, he decided to leave the school. One of his coaches suspected he was on drugs because his behavior was so erratic.

Chip came home, and we realized Chip needed to see a counselor. She advised us to be strong and firm with Chip, and to use "tough love." When we did, Chip broke down. It was a wonderful moment. We thought we had finally gotten through to him.

The next semester, Chip enrolled at the University of Maryland. It looked like he had his life turned around, but a few months later, he started exhibiting that bizarre behavior again. One time when Chip came home, we found a plastic bag of drugs. At first, he said he was holding it for a friend. But I told him, "Chip, remember, I'm your mother. I know when you're not telling the truth." Then he said he "had tried it." He also told us he was seeing a drug counselor, and in fact, we talked to the counselor several times. We thought he was getting the help he needed. I think I was like many parents today . . . pretty naive. I didn't know much about drugs and how they affected people. I know a lot more now.

But in July of 1990, Chip took twenty-one thousand dollars to Miami to buy cocaine. He spent several days there trying to negotiate a deal with several men, but it didn't work out. After he gave up, he made a fatal mistake. He asked one of these men to drive him to the airport. On the way there, these men took him to a road near Biscayne Bay and shot him. He died there.

After he died, I talked to the federal drug agent in Miami. I asked him, "How can this boy be in my family, stay with me, and I would not know he was on cocaine?"

The agent told me, "It is a very private drug. It's not a social drug. You could be working with someone every day side by side. He could have a cocaine habit, and you would never know it."

I hope parents will let their children communicate openly with them. I tell troubled children, "You need to talk to your parents," and many of them say, "But they'll get so mad at me!" Parents need to let their children talk. They need to open the lines of communication and let the children talk openly to them. I think it's really important for parents to read and to be educated about drugs and what's going on in our high schools today.

It's very hard to look at our family albums and see the pictures of our kids growing up. It's easy to blame myself for what happened. Recently I heard somebody say, "When something bad happens, you can't take all the blame any more than you can take all the credit when something good happens." Children make choices. Sometimes those are in line with their parents' wishes and model; sometimes they aren't. We need to cling to the Lord, to pray for our children, and to let them make those choices.

The day that Chip died, I began to learn what it means to "die to self." I know I have a loving Savior who meets all my needs. I have *a joy that I never thought I'd have again. I still have a purpose—that's why I'm here. God still has more for me to do. That's the most important thing in my entire life.*

Gary Cuozzo

Former NFL quarterback; father of Chip Cuozzo

I went down to Miami to identify Chip's body, and I lay in bed that night and cried out to God. The next week, my other children went to Maryland to get his things, and they found a stack of letters to me that—typical of Chip's life—he had never mailed. As I read these letters, I learned that Chip had a very real faith in God, but he was very, very insecure.

I picked up these letters and read them, and my tears fell on them. I had known him for twenty-two years, but I now found out what was really inside him. One of them read: "The truth is that I did not want to try and fail, so I pretended not to care and in this way I would never have to suffer a letdown . . ."

Another letter told of his pain and fear: "I cannot overcome my inferior, embarrassed, shy, negative opinion of myself." Still another read: "I thought if I was supposed to be this king that all the other people were telling me I was, I either fooled the crud out of all of them, or that one day all of a sudden I would be 'Joe Confidence.'" Chip also wrote: "I love everyone deep down and hurt more than you could ever imagine."

I have a letter from Chip when he was in the eighth grade which says how senseless it is for people to use drugs. So early in his life, he saw . . . he knew what drugs would do to people. But two years later, he was on the varsity team, and the pressures grew. He started to drink, and he came home drunk one night. He was confused. Life was complicated. He called himself "the most shy, insecure person in the world."

It was obvious that Chip was taking steroids during his senior year in high school when he gained so much muscle in such a short period of time. And I think taking the steroids eventually led to his cocaine abuse. I don't think there is any direct link between steroids and cocaine. The correlation seems to be the "risk personality": Somebody who would take the risk of using steroids would also be likely to use cocaine to feel good and strong.

Our society expects athletes to be tough: "Real men don't cry. Real men are tough." If you pick up this week's sports magazine, you'll see men scowling at the camera, but that's not the whole picture. These men are real people with real feelings, not mean, tough cartoon characters. We need to be careful what kind of expectations we put on athletes. We need to let them be people.

Another problem today is that peer pressure is negative. When I was a kid, peer pressure was positive. It was good to make good grades; it was good to be a good athlete. But in the sixties and seventies, I saw a change. It became more fashionable not to care about these values. Kids today are victimized by our culture which robs them of good values. The cigarette and beer industries spend billions of dollars to convince young people that fun and athletics are associated with smoking and drinking. There's something about these ads which draws the kids' attention. Today, you see kids make decisions to smoke and drink at a very young age, but these decisions are peer decisions to be accepted, not because they have thought through them.

The number one influence in kids' lives is peer pressure. It used to be parents and church, but not anymore. Decisions were easier when you had parents and church forming opinions.

Chip's letters have given me a ministry. Otherwise, I would have very little to say because I wouldn't understand the pain that was in Chip's life. The letter that meant the most to me is the one that says: "God is the only thing that ever did, does now, and ever will matter. I never doubted God or His Son Jesus Christ."

Chip's letter has comforted and encouraged me. Like him, I never doubted that God has done a work in my heart to make me believe the reality of the cross of Jesus Christ. That's my hope. The only hope we have is Christ.

I hope parents will pray for their kids daily, and try to communicate without losing their composure. Anger breaks the communication bridge, but kids desperately need to feel understood. It is very difficult not to be angry with stupid decisions, but I'll tell you, nothing good ever comes from anger. Try to maintain open lines of communication.

Michael was a jock. In high school he was called the next Bo Jackson or Deion Sanders. He was an All-State running back, an All-State guard on the basketball team, and an All-District sprinter. He led his baseball team in home runs and stolen bases. The college scouts drooled when they mentioned his name!

He received thirty-eight offers for scholarships, and he chose his state university. He was billed as the athlete who would bring a conference championship—and maybe a national championship. He had a terrific freshman season, but he was injured in the third game the next year. Michael lost a half step and was never the same football player. But his love of sports didn't disappear. His accomplishments in football were equalled by his heroics in baseball. By the time he graduated, Michael was looking at a promising baseball career.

Virtually everybody expected Michael to be in the minors for only a year or so, but the pitchers were tougher than he expected. He hit only a dozen home runs and batted only .247. Not bad for a rookie season, but not exactly major league material. He—and everyone else—had expected more. "Next year!" Michael told his family and friends. "Next year!"

But the next year was no different, and the next year too. Slowly the dream died. He knew he wasn't going to make it.

Michael had become a Christian at a Fellowship of Christian Athletes camp when he was a freshman in high school. His faith was important to him. In fact, the high school and college coaches and baseball scouts liked his pleasant demeanor. He had a very positive *impact on other players. Several became Christians because Michael told them about Christ. When his dreams of the major leagues, MVP, and the World Series began to fade, he decided to pursue youth ministry.*

A couple of years of Bible school helped sharpen his skills and motivation to serve the Lord. Again he had loads of offers to join a team, but this time it was a church staff as youth minister. As he had done in virtually everything he had tried, Michael was a big success. The students loved hearing stories about sports, and they enjoyed hearing how Christ was relevant to every aspect of their lives.

Eight years later, Michael had married and had two daughters. Denominational leaders asked him to speak at state conventions. Sports had become a platform for a wonderful ministry. It all collapsed.

One day in a staff meeting, Michael began to shake uncontrollably. The church secretary said, "You must have that flu everybody has been getting. Why don't you go home and get some rest?"

But the pastor could tell that Michael didn't have a fever. He had seen this kind of reaction before. A couple of days later, he asked Michael to come to his study. "How are you feeling, Michael?" he asked. "You looked pretty bad Monday morning."

"I'm fine now. Thanks for asking."

The pastor sighed heavily. He wanted to stop right there, but he knew he needed to keep probing. "Michael, my dad was an alcoholic. He was a highly respected man in the community, but he was still an alcoholic. I remember one time he tried to quit, and for several days, he . . . well, he shook. Kind of like you did the other day." The pastor waited for a response.

Michael's eyes darted. His breathing became quick and shallow. "I don't know what you mean." A few seconds seemed like a few hours, then Michael blurted, "I guess I do know what you mean! Are you saying . . . Are you accusing me of being an alcoholic just because I shook when I had the flu?"

The pastor wasn't sure his guess was right, but he was willing to risk their relationship in order to get to the truth. He decided not to argue. "Michael, I'm not accusing you of anything. I'm your friend, and I'm trying to be friend enough to ask you a hard question." He took a deep breath. Both men knew what was coming. "Michael, are you drinking or using some kind of drug?"

Without a word, Michael stood up and strode quickly toward the door. The pastor heard the door shut. Then there was silence.

The secretary walked to the pastor's door. Unaware of what had happened, she said, "That was a short meeting. I guess Michael was in a hurry to get to another appointment." The pastor said nothing, but he wondered if he had done the right thing. All day he questioned himself and wondered what would happen next. His stomach was in knots.

The next afternoon, Michael called and asked the pastor to meet him at a park. "Certainly. I'll be there in a few minutes," he responded. Both of them had sweaty palms as the pastor's car pulled into the parking lot and he joined Michael on a bench. Both sat silently for a minute, then Michael said softly, "It's been going on since college." He swallowed a lump in his throat and said, "I've tried to quit a thousand times." He broke down and cried.

Over the next few days, the pastor proved to be a true friend to Michael. He helped him find a treatment center. He helped him explain his addiction to his wife. And he helped him begin the long process of recovery. There seemed to be a million questions—monumental questions—about Michael's secrecy, his position as a pastor, and his future as a father, husband, and Christian leader.

This story points to a recurring fact in countless cases of substance abuse: nobody wants to believe it's true. Michael was a star, a hero, and a model Christian leader. But he couldn't face his dependency on alcohol. He had hidden his drinking from everybody. The signs were there, but his wife just didn't want to believe that her hero, her protector, and the father of her children was an alcoholic. There was too much to lose.

And the other people at church? Michael could always explain his bloodshot eyes by saying he had been up late talking to young people or flying in from a speaking engagement. The "house of cards" fell only when one person had the courage to ask for the truth.

Today Michael is doing exceptionally well. The tenacity and

discipline he had as a sports star served him well in overcoming old habits and learning new behaviors. He is an even more effective leader today because his natural skills have been tempered by the fires of failure, heartache, soul-searching honesty, and the process of rebuilding his life and relationships.

All of us recognize the media's caricature of an alcoholic: slurred speech and decreased motor skills. But many parents and coaches have difficulty seeing the more subtle patterns of alcohol or drug abuse, especially because these patterns usually develop so gradually and because we don't want to believe they really exist. Perhaps the best way to learn how you can tell if someone is using drugs is to learn the stages of addiction. Not everyone who uses drugs or alcohol is an addict, but that fact doesn't lessen the need for us to identify people who are in the addictive process so we can help them reverse the course of their lives.

Different authorities label the stages of drug and alcohol use in different ways. The description we use is adapted from *Rapha's Twelve-Step Program for Overcoming Chemical Dependency*.[1]

STAGE 1: EXPERIMENTING

The user:

- responds to the encouragement of others to try alcohol or drugs
- is excited about doing something new and possibly forbidden
- typically uses "light stuff" such as alcohol or marijuana
- experiences euphoria with few negative consequences
- learns to enjoy using

STAGE 2: SEEKING

The user:

- likes the feeling of being high and uses alcohol or drugs to fit in socially
- establishes limits on use (for example: two beers, or three joints, or three sniffs, or taking prescription drugs "only as directed")

- sometimes goes over the limit and experiences negative consequences
- is usually in control of the amount of alcohol or drugs used, though there may be some problems at home, school, or work because of drug or alcohol use

STAGE 3: OBSESSING

The user:

- becomes preoccupied with getting high
- regularly breaks the self-imposed rules established in stage 2
- begins to lose control of aspects of his life due to preoccupation with drugs
- feels confusion, guilt, and shame over increased drug use; projects blame for behavior onto others; rationalizes, justifies, and minimizes painful feelings and inappropriate behavior

STAGE 4: CONSUMING

The user:

- is consumed by the substance even as he consumes it and needs it just to feel normal
- blames others for the consequences of drug use and considers avenues of escape such as moving out of town, leaving the family, or committing suicide
- experiences deteriorating mental, spiritual, and physical health
- experiences withdrawal symptoms when he tries to stops using

For some people, progress through these stages takes years, and some can arrest the slide through sheer will power. Other people, however, seem to sprint down the addictive path of destruction. The type of drug, too, determines the rapidity of the process. Virtually all authorities report that people can become physiologically addicted to crack cocaine from the first instance of use.

Counselors who work with chemically dependent people observe a wide variety of characteristics associated with drug and alcohol use. As a person progresses through the stages of addiction, these characteristics become more pronounced.

RELATIONAL

The user displays:

- changes in circle of friends (new friends are users; they may or may not hide their use of substances)
- unwillingness to bring new friends home or even talk about them
- unexplained absences from home
- preference for heavy metal or acid rock music

BEHAVIORAL

The user exhibits:

- mood swings, secretiveness, withdrawal
- unpredictable behavior (explosions of anger, lying, fear, and shame)
- problems at school or work
- changes in sleep patterns
- changes in eating habits
- problems with money
- delusional thinking or hallucinations
- changes in activities (social, recreational, hobbies)
- impulsiveness and poor judgment
- lack of motivation and discipline
- possession of drug paraphernalia

PHYSICAL

The user experiences:

- increasing health problems, especially respiratory and gastro-intestinal
- nausea or vomiting
- frequent drowsiness

- increasingly poor memory, glazed expression
- poor grooming habits
- vision or eye problems such as constricted pupils, dilated pupils, non-reactive pupils, inability to track with eyes, or bloodshot eyes[2]

Note: These physical effects can also be caused by medical problems, so parents, coaches, and friends should not jump to conclusions if someone exhibits these characteristics.

KEEP YOUR EYES OPEN

It takes tremendous courage to ask questions when we really don't want to hear the answers. But we are foolish to keep our heads buried in the proverbial sand. Here are some patterns to observe.

Progression Look for the progression of any of the characteristics in each category (relational, behavioral, and physical). These may occur so gradually that you don't notice, so compare current behavior to past behavior for differences. Sometimes drug use can escalate overnight. In that case, we are tempted to think, "This is out of character for him! Surely he'll get back to normal in a day or so." And he may, but the new behavior at least needs to be acknowledged if not addressed immediately.

Remember, adolescents normally change dramatically and erratically during this phase of their lives. So be careful not to jump to conclusions.

Secrecy In developing their own identities, adolescents often become private people. That is fine—up to a point. If a young person won't give a satisfactory explanation of suspicious behavior, it is wise to be cautious. Explain that you want to have a relationship based on respect and trust. That means that some things are private, but those that affect both of you need to be adequately discussed.

Escaping Problems Drinking or using becomes much more

dangerous when the person begins to use the substance to escape problems. This may begin in an effort to block the pain or disappointment of a particularly difficult problem, but if it "works," the teen will likely do it again for less painful problems. This pattern continues until the person tries to escape virtually all problems. Of course, it quickly becomes self-perpetuating because drug and alcohol use creates its own problems.

Mood Swings Drinking or taking drugs to escape problems usually creates wide mood swings. As escape becomes more prevalent, the person's healthy coping skills atrophy. New problems seem more hopeless, and depression and anger deepen. Drug use provides relief and even euphoria, followed by a crash. Drug-induced depression is coupled with the hopelessness of lost coping skills and strained relationships. At that point, even normal problems seems like mountains. So escape is even more attractive, and the cycle of depression and euphoria continues.

Tolerance One of the most significant indicators of drug and alcohol dependency is increased tolerance. In the drinking culture, it is a mark of bravado to "drink people under the table," to "have a hollow leg," and to "hold your liquor." But the capacity to consume great quantities of alcohol or drugs with minimal effect is a sign that the body is becoming acclimated to the substance. Eventually the bodily systems are dependent on the substance to function "normally." Abuse has then become addiction.

Frank was famous for his ability to drink. He bought a half gallon of vodka every Friday afternoon and drank half of it on Friday night and the other half on Saturday night. He got high, but he never passed out or lost control. His friends were in awe of Frank's ability to consume alcohol. "Frank can't even get drunk on beer anymore!" they said in awe. They didn't realize that his liver was being damaged, he has a greater risk of heart disease and gastrointestinal problems, and that the alcohol was literally killing him. If they did, their awe might turn to pity and concern.

CLINICAL DEFINITIONS

Clinicians make a distinction between substance *dependence*, which is an addiction, and substance *abuse*, which is less severe. These terms describe the use of a drug that impairs social and occupational functioning and produces a psychological dependence. Both of these are listed under the category of Psychoactive Substance Abuse Disorders in the *Diagnostic and Statistical Manual*.[3]

Dependence, or addiction, is defined by the presence of three or more of the following symptoms for at least one month.

- The person uses more of the substance or uses it for a longer time than intended.
- The person acknowledges excessive use of the substance and may have tried to reduce it but has been unable to do so.
- Much of the person's time is spent in efforts to obtain the substance or recover from its effects.
- The person is intoxicated or suffering from withdrawal symptoms at times when responsibilities need to be met, as in school or work.
- The person has given up or reduced his or her participation in many activities because of the use of the substance.
- Problems in health, social relationships, and psychological functioning occur.
- Tolerance develops, requiring larger doses (at least a 50 percent increase) of the substance to produce the desired effect.
- Withdrawal symptoms develop when the person stops ingesting substances or reduces the amount.
- The person uses the substance to relieve withdrawal symptoms. (For example, drinking alcohol early in the morning because withdrawal symptoms are appearing.)

Substance abuse, which is less severe than dependence, is defined as the presence of at least one of these traits.

- Continued use despite persistent or recurrent social, occupational, psychological, or physical problems caused by or exacerbated by use of the psychoactive substance.

- Recurrent use in situations in which use is physically hazardous. For example, driving while intoxicated.[4]

Psychologist and author Les Parrott III describes four common types of drug abusers in his book *Helping the Struggling Adolescent*.

The Experimenter   This adolescent experiments with drug use to gain acceptance and be "in the know." His use is short-term and infrequent.

The Recreationist   This young person uses drugs to share pleasurable experiences with friends, not to achieve a mood or mental effect.

The Seeker   This adolescent seeks an altered state and uses drugs and/or alcohol regularly to achieve a sedated or intoxicated effect.

The Drug Head   This is a sick adolescent who has moved on to regular use of hard drugs like cocaine or heroin. He or she is addicted.[5]

As we have seen, many factors contribute to an individual's experimentation and progression of use, abuse, and dependence. The support and encouragement of family members can give young people the strength and wisdom they need to never start—or to stop—their slide into the black hole of abuse and addiction. But family members can also have the opposite effect; they can contribute to the stress and irresponsibility that grease the skids.

FAMILY MEMBERS OF ALCOHOLICS OR USERS

Drug and alcohol abuse affect family members and friends. Years ago, counselors who worked with families of alcoholics noticed certain patterns of behavior in members. Studies show that children of alcoholics are more likely than those from non-alcoholic homes to become alcoholics themselves. Experts debate about the existence of a "genetic link" and the effects of parental modeling, but whatever the cause, those from alcoholic homes need to be aware of the increased risk of their own use of drugs or alcohol.[6]

The patterns of behavior for family members vary, but these characteristics are typical:

- a lack of objectivity about the family's problems (minimizing, denial, etc.)
- a warped sense of responsibility, feeling the need to fix others' problems
- being easily controlled by others' anger, self-pity, silence, and demands
- trying to control others in these same ways
- unresolved hurt and anger
- intense feelings of guilt and shame
- feeling isolated, lonely, and afraid of authority figures
- fear of angry, demanding people
- living for the approval of others, and feeling crushed when they disapprove
- the need to find someone to blame for personal and family problems, even if the person blamed is yourself
- feeling like a victim
- feeling misunderstood and abandoned even though you try to please people

Following are two questionnaires that will help you assess your—or a family member's or friend's—risk level for chemical dependency and codependency.

ARE YOU CHEMICALLY DEPENDENT?[7]

If you suspect you have a substance abuse problem, take this questionnaire by yourself then ask a friend or family member to take it with you in mind.

If you suspect a family member or friend has a problem, take this test with that person in mind.

Yes   No

☐   ☐   1. Do you lose time from work or school because of drinking or using drugs?

☐   ☐   2. Is drinking or using drugs making your home life unhappy?

☐   ☐   3. Do you drink or use drugs because you feel shy and insecure around people?

☐   ☐   4. Is drinking or using drugs affecting your reputation?

☐   ☐   5. Have you ever felt remorse after drinking or using?

☐   ☐   6. Have you gotten into financial difficulties as a result of drinking or using drugs?

☐   ☐   7. Do you seek out unsuitable companions or an inferior environment when drinking or using drugs?

☐   ☐   8. Does your drinking or using make you careless about your family's welfare?

☐   ☐   9. Has your ambition decreased since you've been drinking or using?

☐   ☐   10. Do you crave a drink or high at a definite time and on a daily basis?

☐   ☐   11. Do you want a drink or high the morning after you've drunk heavily or taken drugs?

☐   ☐   12. Does drinking or using cause you to have difficulty sleeping?

☐   ☐   13. Has your efficiency decreased since you've been drinking or using drugs?

☐   ☐   14. Is drinking or using jeopardizing your job or schoolwork?

☐   ☐   15. Do you drink or use to escape worries, trouble, or a feeling of rejection?

Yes	No	
☐	☐	16. Do you drink or use drugs alone?
☐	☐	17. Have you ever had a complete loss of memory as a result of drinking or using?
☐	☐	18. Has a physician ever treated you for drinking or using drugs?
☐	☐	19. Do you drink or use drugs to build your self-confidence?
☐	☐	20. Have you ever been to a hospital or institution because of drinking or using?

If you answer *yes* to any of these questions, you may have a problem with alcohol or drugs.

If you answer *yes* to any two, chances are you have a problem.

If you answer *yes* to three or more, you definitely have a problem with alcohol or drugs.

ARE YOU A CODEPENDENT? [8]

If you suspect you have the problem of being controlled by other people, take this questionaire. Then ask a trusted friend to take it with you in mind.

If you suspect a family member or friend has a problem, take this test with that person in mind.

Yes	No	
☐	☐	1. Do you often feel isolated and afraid of people, especially authority figures?
☐	☐	2. Have you observed yourself to be an approval-seeker, losing your own identity in the process?
☐	☐	3. Do you feel overly frightened of angry people and criticism?
☐	☐	4. Do you often believe you are a victim in personal and career relationships?

□ □ 5. Do you sometimes think you have an overdeveloped sense of responsibility that makes you more concerned with others than with yourself?

□ □ 6. Is it hard for you to look at your own faults and take responsibility for yourself?

□ □ 7. Do you feel guilty when you stand up for yourself instead of giving in to others?

□ □ 8. Are you addicted to excitement?

□ □ 9. Do you confuse love with pity and tend to love people you can pity and rescue?

□ □ 10. Is it hard for you to express feelings, including joy or happiness?

□ □ 11. Do you judge yourself harshly (name-calling, blaming, condemning)?

□ □ 12. Do you have low self-esteem?

□ □ 13. Do you often feel abandoned in relationships?

□ □ 14. Do you tend to be a reactor instead of an initiator?

If you answered *yes* to two of these questions, you have codependent tendencies.

If you answered *yes* to four, chances are you have a problem.

If you answered *yes* to six or more, you definitely have a problem with codependency.

6

FIGHTING BACK!

___

Dal

Ninety-six percent of Americans and 80 percent of the world are influenced by sports in some way. Millions of people read the sports page who never read the Bible. Sports is a fantastic window of opportunity in our society, and One Way 2 Play! is a tool to take advantage of the opportunity sports gives us to talk about the real solution to one of the biggest problems in our culture.

Right now, we have school administrators who call us and ask if we have anything that will help them. I hope school administrators and school boards will use One Way 2 Play! to reach their students and provide a strong, positive environment of education, account- ability, and recovery. One Way 2 Play! works because it is a comprehensive program which stresses individual responsibility as well as peer group accountability. We are excited about the reports we hear from teams and schools across the country! It is my dream and my goal to have FCA and One Way 2 Play! on every campus in America by the year 2000.

It breaks my heart when I hear of eight-, nine-, ten-, and eleven- year-olds becoming delivery boys and girls for drug dealers, or when I hear that these children are selling crack capsules back to the dealers for thirty-five cents each in order to make some money. This opens the door for them to get more and more deeply involved in this destructive trade. Some of these young men and women will become addicts. Many will ruin their lives. And some will die.

I'd like to see hundreds of professional and college athletes doing school assemblies and speaking at churches to be role models and to share strong testimonies of how Jesus Christ changes lives. And even high school athletes can have a profound impact on their classmates and on junior high students if they will speak about and model their commitment to Christ. Let's have an impact on the junior football programs, Little League, and youth soccer programs. Coaches and athletes at all levels can make a difference—a big difference—on young lives.

Marge had been a teacher at the junior high school for fourteen years. Her husband, Will, had been assistant football coach and math teacher at the high school for several years and was eventually made head coach. Marge saw the drug problem every day in her students—bloodshot eyes, runny noses from sniffing inhalants, kids meeting older kids after school to buy and sell, lack of attention in class, and other obvious signs. Will had seen it, too, but he focused on the "good kids" on his team. He knew that some of them drank beer and let them know he didn't approve, but he really laid down the law about smoking cigarettes. He didn't want anything hurting their breathing and endurance. Will didn't think he needed to say anything about smoking anything else. He was wrong.

The team had a good chance of winning the district championship. There was speculation that they might get farther than any team from that high school had ever gone in the state playoffs. They won their first three games of the year. One of them was against the previous year's district champs. Things were looking really good! The next two weeks were against pushovers, or at least that's what they seemed. Will's team won those games as well. Now their record was 5-0. A good start for a championship year!

But late Sunday night on the weekend after the third win, the police called Will. "Coach, we've got two of your players down here. They asked if they could call you instead of their parents. Can you come down to the station?"

"Okay. What did they do? Steal something? Are they charged with anything?"

"Yes, Coach. They're charged with possession with intent to distribute a controlled substance."

"Drugs?" The coach was incredulous.

"Coach, they tried to sell crack to an undercover agent. I'm sorry to tell you that. Can you come to the station?"

"I'll be right there," the coach groaned.

The boys were booked and released on bail. Shock waves rippled through the town, the school, and especially the team. The boys were suspended until after the trial. The team would face several games—and maybe the rest of the season—without two of its best players.

Marge and Will had many long conversations the days after the boys were arrested. "I can't believe those boys would do such a stupid thing!" Will kept saying. Their reactions gradually turned from shock to a commitment to do something about the drug problem in their community. "But how do we start?" Marge wondered. "The problem seems so big . . . so hopeless. What can we do?"

Some pieces of the puzzle were already in place. The school had a DARE program, the school counselors worked with problem students, and some youth ministers and parents were speaking out clearly and strongly about drug- and alcohol-related issues. These efforts were good, but they didn't seem to reach many of the at-risk students.

Marge and Will committed themselves to helping establish other resources for user education, prevention, and recovery.

EDUCATION AND SUPPORT

School officials recognize the devastating effects of drugs and alcohol and have instituted programs to inform and motivate students to avoid using them. But parental modeling is a more powerful influence, so educating parents must be a focus too. Mental health organizations (both state and private) and organizations such as Mothers Against Drunk Driving (MADD) provide literature and speakers for civic groups, clubs, and church groups. Parents need to understand the complexities of the influences on young people, even elementary age children, in such areas as:

- why young people experiment with drugs and alcohol
- entry points such as wine coolers and inhalants
- the warning signs
- effects on the body, motivation, and relationships
- the progression of addiction
- prevention techniques
- intervention techniques
- treatment and post-treatment care

Parents shouldn't simply be put on a guilt trip when a child drinks or uses drugs. Most are very conscientious and want to help their children any way they can. But they need to seek help for themselves first. Any program for educating parents needs to also be an open door for helping hurting parents too.

Some people criticize drug education programs by calling them "scare tactics," but the truth sometimes *is* scary. We are foolish to beat around the bush about this crucial issue. Youth don't respond to mere concepts and theories. They need flesh-and-blood examples and face-to-face contact with people who care about them and will ask them hard questions. We can't just wish the problem away. The best programs are those that put a respected person in front of young people to tell his own story and elicit a commitment from them to make good decisions. The best programs also get young people talking so they can share their hurts and hopes with each other and receive the support of their peers.

LOVE

The message young people desperately need to hear is, "You are valuable! You are loved!" The Scriptures teach us about our value. We were lost and without hope because of our sin, apathy, and rebellion against God, but Jesus Christ died to pay for our sins, and He rose from the grave to give us new life. In the first chapter of Paul's letter to the Ephesian believers, he reminds them that they have been chosen by God, adopted by Him into His family, forgiven of all their sins, and sealed in this new relationship with Him by the Spirit of God. Adolescents who wonder "Who am I?" need to hear this declaration of identity in Christ.

This message gives us a connection—it gives our lives meaning. Some of us feel loved and accepted by our families, but some of us don't. We may have been abandoned or abused by others, but Christ will never leave us or forsake us. He is consistently loving and accepting. And He is with us all the time, even when we don't feel His presence.

We also have connections in the family of God. Our earthly brothers and sisters may ridicule us or betray us, but those who truly love God love one another.

FORGIVENESS

The forgiveness God offers us is genuinely "good news." We have all done things we regret, but many of us have seen blame and denial modeled as responses to sin, and these only produce more sinful behavior. Old-time preachers of God's grace used to say, "God is the God of second chances . . . and third chances, and fourth chances, and . . . " Guilt and shame gnaw at our security and erode our relationships, but the forgiveness of God washes us clean. Then we can forgive those who have hurt us instead of harboring bitterness toward them. We may savor that bitterness because we think that someday we can get revenge, but the only person we hurt is ourselves. Paul directed the Ephesians to "[forgive] one another just as God in Christ also forgave you" (Eph. 4:32).

But forgiveness doesn't mean we let people do anything they want to us. We also grow in our wisdom and perception about people, and we learn to speak the truth, to say no when it's appropriate, and to find sources of spiritual and emotional growth and renewal.

HOPE

Young people need a sense of hope, and the message of Christ is preeminently one of hope and purpose. God *does* have a plan for our lives. He *does* care about us and our circumstances. He *will* give us wisdom and strength when we need them. But this doesn't mean we will understand His plan and purpose at every point along the way. God is inscrutable; we can't understand all He does. We have to trust that He will bring us through difficulties.

SIN OR SICKNESS?

In schools and in the churches, there is debate about whether addictions are "sin" or "sickness." Most secular counselors teach that alcoholism or drug addiction is a disease, but many Christians point to bad choices and call it sin. Many believers think that calling addiction a disease promotes irresponsibility. The argument over genetic predisposition has not resolved the problem. It has only divided the two sides more sharply.

We believe that addiction begins as a sin, a choice to get high or escape, an attempt to resolve life's problems apart from the will of God. The Scriptures clearly teach that drunkenness is a sin (Eph. 5:18, Prov. 20:1). Drinking is not specifically condemned except in matters of personal conscience (Rom. 14:22-23); when drinking is a bad example for others; and when it actually influences others' decisions (Rom. 14:1-21).

By the time drug or alcohol use progresses to an addiction, however, the person's condition has many characteristics of a disease, such as the following.

- There is an identifiable, external cause.
- There are physical symptoms.
- It has a predictable progression.
- It harms the person physiologically.
- It is treatable.[1]

These physiological and medical consequences are quite real.

Indeed, unless God miraculously intervenes, medical treatment is required for detoxification. But the initial cause is a behavioral and spiritual problem in which a person turns to substances to meet his needs. The *body* needs medical treatment, the *behavior* needs to be changed by acquiring new skills and patterns of responses, and the *soul* needs repentance, forgiveness, and intimacy with God.

PREVENTION TOOLS

You Contact with and modeling by parents, coaches, teachers, and peers can elicit specific commitments. These can then be reinforced in countless ways to build character and establish positive patterns of behavior.

Commitment Sheet The One Way 2 Play—Drug Free! commitment sheet (reproduced on page 172) can be presented by the Huddle coach (or Sunday school teacher, youth minister, or group leader) as a statement of intent to avoid alcohol and drugs. Signing this sheet is a public demonstration of this commitment.

The commitment sheet also includes a hand signal which students can use to remind each other of their commitment to live and play drug-free. Other reinforcements to commitment are One Way 2 Play—Drug Free! T-shirts, patches, posters, and bumper stickers (see the order form at the back of this book). Others might ask what the slogan means, and the teen can tell why he or she has chosen to follow Christ and be drug-free. They are great conversation starters!

Contracts Contracts can be useful for at-risk young people or those who need to stop their slide down addiction's slope. These need to be specific and enforceable to be effective. If they are overused, vague in their rewards and consequences, or not enforced, they actually have a negative effect and hinder the development of internal motivation and positive behaviors. Contracts can be used by coaches or youth ministers, but they are most appropriate in the context of families.

If you choose to use a contract, ask the adolescent to list several specific rewards and consequences she thinks would be appropriate. (Young people are often much tougher on themselves than parents would be. You may need to negotiate these to be sure they are appropriate and fair.) Then write the contract up, listing the commitment, the rewards for good behavior, and the consequences for bad choices. Here is an example.

CONTRACT

In order to be a responsible family member, I will:

1. Not experiment with any type of drug, including cigarettes.
2. Not ride in a car with anyone who has been drinking or using.
3. Date only people who are "clean."

My rewards will be:

1. After six months, an increase in my allowance to seven dollars per week.
2. After one year, extended car privileges.
3. After graduation, a weekend with my friends at the beach.

Consequences include:

1. First offense, grounded for three days.
2. Second offense, grounded for two weeks, and no social contact for two weeks with whoever participated.
3. Third offense, driving privileges withheld for two months, grounded for three weeks, no social contact for three weeks with whoever participated.

_____   _____
Teen   Date

_____   _____
Father   Date

_____   _____
Mother   Date

At-risk youth need to be held accountable on a regular, scheduled basis or the contract will be a farce. For instance, each Sunday night the parents may call a family meeting (or a meeting with only the at-risk son or daughter) and ask, "Did you uphold the contract this week?" The son or daughter then responds.

The contract will need to be amended over time to compensate for changes in age, the ability to drive, and changes in rewards and privileges. Also, if the contract simply isn't working, the problem needs to be identified and a remedy sought. The parents may not be faithful in following through with the weekly check-up, or the teen may be lying, or peer pressure may be overwhelming.

The contract may be a way to help the adolescent deal with peer pressure. He may say, "I can't. If I did, I'd be grounded for three weeks. It's not worth it!"

Activities Positive, healthy activities are some of the best prevention tools available. Sports, for example, provide young people with the opportunity to get exercise and learn to play on a team. The responsibility they feel to perform well for their teammates may be enough to help them say no to drugs.

The Fellowship of Christian Athletes takes this environment a step farther by encouraging coaches to communicate biblical principles and provide meaningful interaction and modeling in their Huddles. Huddles take time and energy for coaches and participants alike, but they may be the best environment young people experience all week.

Youth groups often plan fun activities in addition to their regular meetings. These activities build relationships and make it easier to talk about the things that really matter.

Some communities recognize events that foster irresponsible behavior and offer alternatives. In one town, some parents and church leaders realized that the annual prom had become an all-night drinking party, so with the input of students, they created an alternative called Project Prom. This event begins immediately following the prom, and it is probably the biggest event in town every year. A ballroom is extravagantly decorated. Local merchants donate merchandise to be given away, a good band plays, everybody gets T-shirts commemorating the event, and the party goes on all night with good, clean fun. Project Prom takes a lot of effort, but it shows students that they can have a great time without drugs and alcohol and the behaviors which often accompany their use: premarital sex, date rape, sexually transmitted diseases, pregnancy, vandalism, alcohol-related car accidents, and a host of other things that young people always think will happen to "the other guy."

Music Music is a big part of the youth culture, and it can build or destroy. We don't need to give examples of secular music—you already know what's out there—but Christian music has made great strides in the last few years. Some outstanding artists and groups have styles which appeal to youth today, and their messages are "light in the darkness" of most secular music. There is some controversy about the legitimacy of some Christian groups, and it is always wise to ask questions and be observant, but we recommend the vast majority of contemporary Christian music because it communicates strong, Christ-centered values and behaviors. Concerts by Christian artists are another wholesome activity young people can enjoy.

INTERVENTION

When we find out people are using drugs or alcohol, we confront them with the consequences of their behavior, and sometimes that is enough for them to change. But remember, they are drinking or using to meet a significant need or to escape from a deep hurt. They often cling to the hope that drinking or using will somehow give them relief and happiness, and as we have seen, if they are truly addicted, their bodies have become physiologically dependent on the drug. They *can't* quit without help—either medical assistance or the supernatural work of God—to overcome their addiction.

Usually, family members and close friends protect users from the consequences of their behavior. A mother blames her own lack of attention for her daughter's drinking, and so never confronts her. A father gives his son money he knows will be spent on drugs because he feels guilty for the divorce. A sister fears the explosions of anger that erupt any time the user is confronted, so she never says anything about the money habitually missing from her purse. A friend calls to tell an employer that his buddy is sick and can't come to work when the buddy is high on grass.

But users must face and experience the natural consequences of their bad choices and irresponsible behavior if they are to be motivated to change. This is a painful and difficult course of action, especially for those of us who have spent years protecting users from the consequences of their behavior. Some may even accuse us of being unloving in letting them experience consequences, but this is the most loving thing we can do for them. Without facing reality, users will probably continue their self-destructive ways. We can agree with them that their needs are valid, but we must convince them they are trying to meet those needs in harmful ways.

In the early stages of trying to relate to an addict or an abuser, most of us try to reason with them. That doesn't work, so we plead. That doesn't work either, so we threaten to leave them or punish them in some way. Nothing changes. We feel angry for being controlled by this person, and we feel guilty for being so angry. The other person isn't changing, but we are—for the worse!

When a person's behavior is destroying himself and others, and he is unresponsive to normal communication, an intervention may be in order. In an intervention, the person is confronted without warning by those who have authority in his life. Clear choices and consequences are laid out, and the addict's response is honored— one way or the other. This form of confrontation can be the last and best hope of helping a person change, but it needs careful and thorough preparation.

Step One Ask an experienced person, a pastor, or a counselor to be the facilitator who will help each person understand and fulfill his or her role.

Step Two Have the facilitator call together those with any authority over the person, such as the school counselor, parents, teachers and coaches, and siblings. (In the case of an adult, invite the boss, pastor, and a non-drinking or non-using friend.)

Step Three Communicate to everyone participating the goals and the process of intervention. Have each person prepare (in writing or at least in outline form) a three-minute statement for the addict or abuser. This statement should be factual, not emotional, and it should describe specific ways the addict's behavior is harming himself and others. If someone does not want to participate, he or she can be excused. When the actual confrontation takes place, every participant must be fully committed to the process.

Step Four Identify and state the goal of intervention (such as admission to a treatment center). Also state clear consequences (such as dismissal from work, suspension from the team or school, denial of funds or allowance, or suspension of driving privileges).

Step Five Prepare everyone for the person's probable re-sponses—violent anger, self-pity, transference of blame, quick agreement just to end the confrontation, or genuine repentance. At the same time, prepare participants to anticipate their own reac-tions to the person's response—anger, guilt, wanting to fix the person and make him feel better, taking the blame for the problem, blaming each other, or withdrawal.

Step Six Invite the addict or abuser to a participating friend's house without telling him what is going on. Cars need to be parked discreetly out of sight. Allow the facilitator to take control when the addict or abuser walks in the door. The facilitator should say something like, "We want to meet with you because we care about you. Please listen to us first, then you can say anything you want to say." Have the facilitator then methodically direct each partici-pant to give their three-minute statements. The goal and consequences are then stated, and the person can make his choice. This is not a time for a lot of discussion. There should be few options. The planning meeting should have narrowed the choices and consequences.

Step Seven Even if the person agrees to take the positive step, the process isn't over. It has only begun! Many will take a step forward but fall back in a day or a week. In that case, the choice needs to be explained and the consequences imposed for non-compliance. The facilitator should carefully monitor the progress of the person to be sure the process is on track. He or she also needs to monitor the progress of the participants over the next couple of days and weeks following the intervention. The trauma of confronting someone is almost as great as the trauma of being confronted. Perhaps the facilitator can meet with the participants as a group a couple of times to affirm and encourage them.

Following is a checklist for intervention.

1. Describe the person's problem and its effects on himself and others.
2. State the goal of intervention.
3. Decide who should be asked to participate.
4. Discuss with the participants:

   - the goal
   - consequences
   - the process
   - each person's role
   - objectives of the three-minute presentations
   - probable responses of the addict or abuser
   - the participants' feelings and reactions before, during, and after the event

5. Decide how you will evaluate the person's progress.
6. Set up a schedule of checkups on the person and the participants:

- one day after
- one week after
- one month after
- three months after
- six months after[2]

An intervention may seem like a drastic measure. It is. It is used when normal means of communication have broken down and proven ineffective. The facilitator plays the role of a coach. He or she selects, trains, and directs each person in the intervention team. Remember, the whole process isn't over when the confronting encounter is over. It lasts until the person becomes stable and healthy, and that will take months.

TREATMENT

All of us need some help from time to time. Coaches call friends for advice about the defense their team will face in the next game. Teachers ask the principal how to work with a problem student. Parents ask the school counselor how to manage a rebellious child. Needing help is not a problem. Problems arise when we need help but don't ask for it. Teenagers with alcohol or drug problems often don't ask for help until they are far down the road in their destructive pattern of use. A wide range of care options are available for adolescents, and each has benefits and limitations. Some people and agencies who can help include the following.

Police   Sometimes, the first step in treatment is not made by the needy person or anybody close to him. The police may take that first step by making an arrest. The adolescent and his parents may want to explain away the behavior, but the police have seen and heard it all before. They won't be snowed by lies, excuses, and accusations.

Friends   Often, the first people to notice we're not doing well are our friends. And they may be the first people we turn to for help.

They are available and they understand, but they usually struggle with the same problems so they may not have many solutions. Friends show their care and their courage when they are willing to tell us the hard truth about our behavior and our needs.

Parents   Most young people don't feel good about telling their parents their problems because they're afraid they will get "chewed on." But some have the wisdom to go to the people who care most about them, and even though the relationship may be strained, they are willing to tell their parents the truth . . . or at least begin to tell them and see how they react! If it goes okay, they will tell them more.

Youth Ministers and Volunteers   Many young people confide in youth ministers or volunteers when they don't feel like they can talk to anybody else. They then get a sympathetic ear and some clear direction.

Coaches   Many young people see coaches as parent figures. This has pros and cons, because the adolescent may believe that everyone in authority is untrustworthy and may be cynical about even the most caring coach. On the positive side, the coach may offer far more attention and encouragement than the player's parents ever have, and this paves the way for open and honest communication.

School Counselors   Truancy and other behavior problems are usually referred to the school counselor, and many times this relationship begins the recovery process.

Professional Counselors   When talks with parents and friends don't seem to help, when performance at school or on the team is hindered, when there has been a traumatic episode like an overdose, or when the abuse has continued over a long period, it is time to seek professional help. Virtually every community has competent counselors who can help, but be careful not to go to just anybody who hangs out a shingle. Look for someone with adequate credentials, expertise in adolescent drug and alcohol recovery, a good reputation in the community, and preferably, a strong commitment to Christ. Not all counselors who say they are Christian counselors do Christian counseling. Some are believers, but their therapy is entirely secular. Look for someone who integrates the truths of God's Word into the treatment plan, who communicates the love and strength of Christ, and who points clients to faith in God, our source of wisdom.

Hospitalization   Drug and alcohol abuse sometimes requires intensive treatment in a medical setting. This setting is becoming more varied and now includes inpatient care, day treatment, partial hospitalization, residential treatment, and intensive outpatient care.

In his book *The Troubled Adolescent*, J. L. White suggests hospitalization be considered if:

- the adolescent has unsuccessfully tried to stop abusing drugs on his or her own
- the adolescent has been unsuccessful in outpatient treatment programs
- there has been an overdose, or the potential for an overdose is strong (for example, the adolescent is mixing street drugs and alcohol)
- medical attention is necessary to control severe withdrawal symptoms
- the adolescent is experiencing suicidal thoughts, bad trips, or flashbacks
- the adolescent's behavior is out of control (for instance, the adolescent is truant, failing school, stealing to obtain drugs, or in denial when confronted with evidence of drug abuse)
- family members are emotionally drained from the roller coaster ride of mood swings, social problems, and arguments that accompany drug abuse[3]

The Fellowship of Christian Athletes has developed a close relationship with Rapha Treatment Centers, one of the nation's leading providers of biblically sound, Christ-centered treatment for psychiatric problems and substance abuse. In hospitals and treatment centers across the country, Rapha offers a continuum of care for adults and adolescents, including books, seminars, intensive outpatient counseling, and partial and inpatient hospital care. Rapha has made its Information Counselors available to the Fellowship of Christian Athletes. If you need assistance as you try to help adolescents in crisis, please call Rapha to get professional direction. Their number is 1-800-383-HOPE.

It has been said, "All that is needed for evil to prevail is for good people to do nothing." The evils of alcohol and drugs in our culture are staggering. They ruin lives and destroy families. They cripple motivation and crush dreams. It's easy to sit back and throw up our hands and say, "What can I do? I'm just one person!" But one person can instill hope in a few, and those few can come up with ideas and resources to educate and equip others, and together we can fight back and make a difference in young lives. By the grace of God, lives can be changed—one at a time.

Kay Yow

Head basketball coach for North Carolina State Wolfpack

Alcohol and drugs give people false security and false confidence. They cause people to be unrealistic and do things they wouldn't do if they weren't taking them. Getting high may feel good for the moment, but sooner or later, people have a lot of regrets. Things are said or done which cause harm to relationships and to athletic performance.

As athletes, it's impossible to be the best you can be if you drink or take drugs. Just impossible. To say you want to excel and to say you want to be the best you can be, and then to take drugs or drink is totally contradictory. You simply can't be your best if you harm your body and your relationships with drugs or alcohol.

Coaches, parents, and leading athletes need to set a good example. You can't tell someone not to do something you're doing yourself. Actions speak louder than words, and people follow our actions, not our words. Alcohol or drugs can destroy your relationships and career. It's just not worth it! It is so sad to see the statistics about drunk drivers, spouse abuse, child abuse, crimes, accidents, and all kinds of other problems which are linked to alcohol and drug use. We need to make wise choices—not necessarily the easy choices—about alcohol and drugs.

7

"YOU CAN DO IT!"

Brent Jones

All-Pro tight end for the San Francisco 49ers

There were times when I saw other players use drugs to get charged up or to get focused for a game. Sometimes I thought about trying it, but really, that was just a passing thought. I became a Christian in high school, and the Lord gave me a tremendous sense of strength and purpose. So really, I had the Lord. I didn't need drugs or alcohol at all.

I played baseball in high school. The farthest thing in my mind at that time was football. I was on the second team in football. In fact, I only played in two games, but through the grace of God, I got a football scholarship to college. All through my career, God has directed me, so I knew I didn't need to rely on drugs to get ready for a game or to come down after a game because God was (and is) the sole reason for my success. Those substances couldn't compare to what God had done for me!

Throughout high school, I had aspirations of playing professional baseball. But because of some injuries, I had my baseball scholarship taken away from me. I figured my only chance to finish school was to play football. Then I got drafted to play in the NFL from a Division II school.

A week after I was drafted by the Pittsburgh Steelers, I got in a car accident. I was put on injured reserve and then released by the Steelers a month or so into the season. I signed with the 49ers as a free agent, and at that point, I was the eighth tight end on the depth chart.

My wife and I have been through a lot of ups and downs together. In our ten years together, we've see the good times of being drafted followed almost immediately by a car accident in which she was hurt pretty badly. Being signed by the Steelers and then being waived two months into the season with almost no hope of getting on with another team. After that, we had the excitement of getting on the 49ers and then having to go through a couple of major knee injuries. At that point, I was on the brink of being cut, but I was kept on. Then miraculously, the starting tight end, John Frank, broke his hand and decided to leave football. He wanted to protect his hand so he could be a surgeon. After John got hurt, the coaching staff made me the starter.

There has been a series of events throughout my career that convinces me that God is in control—even in the discouraging times. I wasn't always sure where I was going, but I knew enough of God's character to trust Him, that He would get me where He wanted me to be. To be honest, I didn't always know that He wanted me to continue in football, but I knew He was there for me. Looking back, I can see God's miraculous hand guiding me and preparing me— even if I couldn't see it at the time.

The toughest time was after the first season with the 49ers when I blew out my knee and had to have my ACL (anterior cruciate ligament) reconstructed in January after a playoff loss to the Vikings. The healing time for that injury was eight to ten months, but training camp started in six months. My knee just wasn't ready, and actually,

I hurt my other knee in the first preseason game in London. Things looked pretty bleak! The 49ers were trying to keep me on the team, but I had two bad knees. The coaches told me I might have to be released from the team. That was really hard to hear. My daughter had just been born only a week before that. So I had to face the prospect of being cut from the team, with a new baby, almost no money, and no job prospects. I had no direction at all. If I wasn't going to be able to play football, I had no idea what I could do at that time. But even then, I knew God had my best interests at heart. I knew I could trust Him to lead me.

Ironically, my college team doctor became the 49ers's doctor at that time, and he convinced the coaching staff to put me on injured reserve. Only a few weeks later, the starting tight end got hurt. The doctor told the coaches that they needed to get me healthy as soon as possible and activate me. I ended up playing a lot that season, catching a few touchdown passes, and playing in my first Super Bowl. In the wisdom and goodness of God, He put that doctor there at the right time for me. I'm thankful for the doctor's willingness to stick up for me, but I'm even more grateful to God for putting him there.

There was a player on the 49ers who had all the talent in the world, but he couldn't quit snorting cocaine. He's been out of the league for five years now, but if he had been straight, he would be one of the stars in the league today. He had great talent, great athletic ability, but even when he saw he was throwing away his career, he still couldn't quit.

If I could talk to young athletes today about drugs and alcohol, I'd tell them: Don't even think about it! If you're a true athlete and you really love playing the game, alcohol and drugs will ruin you! That's the fastest way to destruction. I've seen players wreck their lives and their careers. People who mess with drugs never come out on top. It always catches up with them. I'd tell young athletes that Jesus Christ can fill their lives and give them real meaning and purpose.

Exhilarated . . . peaceful . . . strong . . . happy . . . accepted . . . That's how people feel when they're high. That's why they get high!

Scared . . . hopeless . . . out of control . . . angry . . . ashamed . . . That's how they feel when they crash, or when they realize they can't quit.

Al was a good kid. He made good grades, and he had lots of friends. He was a pretty good defensive back, too, and he hoped to get a scholarship to college someday if he kept playing well. But things weren't good at home. His parents' marriage had been rocky for a long time, and it was getting worse. The fights, the screaming, the slamming doors, the long nights wondering if his dad would come home, hoping he would . . . and hoping he wouldn't.

Al stayed away from home as much as possible. He got a part-time job. That and practice kept him away from the house as much as possible. Being away was a relief, and he could have lived that way without too much problem, except for one thing: His eight-year-old sister couldn't get away. She was stuck there in all the fury. She needed help, but she didn't have anybody to help her. Al felt pangs of guilt every time he thought of her, which was all day, every day.

As the months went by in his junior year, Al was torn between his urge to get away from the house and his desire to care for his sister. He could see the emotions in her eyes when he left for school each morning: sadness, fear, confusion, anger.

For the past year or so, Al had been having a few beers with some of his buddies. Now the stress was getting to him. The buzz helped him relax and laugh. Gradually Al began to have "just one more," because it helped him relax more and forget the pain more. And another one helped even more. And another one. Soon, Al was drinking ten to twelve beers every time he went out with his buddies. They loved it! He told funny stories as they rode around town drinking every weekend.

But one of his friends didn't think all this was so funny. Judy and Al had dated on and off for a couple of years. Even when they weren't dating, they were good friends. Judy had mentioned to him a couple of times that she thought he was drinking too much, but he shrugged it off. "It's nothing," he'd say. Judy wanted to believe that, but other signs told her it was more than "nothing."

The term ended. Judy saw Al after school. "Hey, Al, what grades did you make this term?"

Al tried to put her off. "They're okay. Hey, Jude, I gotta go. See you later, okay?"

But Judy could see the discouragement in his face. "Wait a minute! What do you mean by 'okay'?"

Al bristled. "I mean they're okay! What's your deal, Judy? Are you my mother?"

Judy paused for a few seconds, then looked him in the eye. "I know things are tough for you, Al," she said. "Can we talk a minute?"

Judy's kindness melted Al. "Sure," he said meekly.

The two walked around for over an hour. Judy told him she knew he was drinking more and more. Al knew she wasn't scolding him. She really cared. "Al, you gotta get a better grip on your life," she pleaded. "Your drinking is getting to be a problem." He began to protest, and she interrupted. "I know you aren't an alcoholic . . . yet. But look, you've got problems at home, you're worried about your little sister, you want to get a scholarship to go to college, and now your grades are dying. You had enough stress before you started drinking, and now you've got more than you can handle."

Al stopped walking. He looked intently at Judy and said, "I'll be honest with you. The only time I feel good these days is after I've had a six-pack."

"Or two!" Judy said.

"All right. Two. But don't you see, Judy, it helps me relax."

Judy couldn't let that one pass. "Bull!" she said bluntly.

"What?"

"You heard me. I said, 'Bull!' Drinking helps you escape. You call it 'relaxing.' But people who are relaxed are more productive and less stressed out. You have been less productive and more stressed out."

Al thought about defending himself, but he decided to listen instead. Judy expressed her confidence in him. She listed his good qualities and *her hopes for his future. "You don't want to throw all that away, Al. Please quit drinking."*

Al heaved a deep sigh. "I can't. I can't quit."

Judy became lovingly defiant at Al's hopelessness. "Give me a break, Al! Tell me, who got up at 6:00 A.M. all summer to work out with weights to be stronger and faster this fall? Who keeps a job and schoolwork and football practice and games all going at the same time? Who made the highest grade in the class in two subjects last year?" She paused to let these questions sink in. "You can do it, Al!"

Al had experienced the cycle of drinking so common but so seldom understood by the person caught up in it. The person uses alcohol or drugs to escape or alleviate the pain. Using brings temporary relief, but it creates more complications (secrecy, doubt, financial problems, shame, and strained relationships) and more pain. The higher level of pain increases the desire to use, and more use creates even more complications and pain, and so on. To stop this process, young people need some tools. If somebody told you to build a cabin but you didn't have lumber, a saw, nails, or a hammer, you'd probably feel hopeless. In the same way, many adolescents feel hopeless when they are told "Just say no!" because they don't have the tools to do it. In this chapter, we want to provide some specific tools to help teens avoid starting or stop using alcohol and drugs. We'll look at managing our thoughts, developing a positive identity, setting goals, and handling failure and peer pressure.

The principles in this chapter certainly apply to young people who are in trouble, but they also can apply to parents, coaches, teachers, and leadership students. They can be used as a foundation for helping adolescents, but we can also use them for personal reflection, encouragement, and repentance.

"STINKIN' THINKIN'"

Which comes first: the chicken or the egg? The bad behavior or the bad thought processes? Whichever comes first, poor choices and "stinkin' thinkin'" feed off each other. Some examples include the following.

Black-or-White Thinking "Jerry is the best friend a guy could ever have! He's terrific!" "I can't stand Jerry! He's a first-class jerk!" You would think that these contradictory statements were from two different people, but they aren't. Some of us are hurt badly and we want people around us to be wonderful and kind and strong—and safe. As long as they meet this standard (which they don't, but we convince ourselves they do), we praise them. But when they fall off their pedestal, they are dirty, rotten slime bags!

Some of us see people as *all good* or *all bad*. We are *all in* a relationship or *all out* of it. We are *all for* an idea or a team or anything else or *all against* it. Black-or-white thinking is actually a form of irresponsibility because it lets us avoid difficult decisions in the gray areas of life where we have to analyze the issues, speak the truth, and resolve conflict. That's a lot more difficult than thinking someone is all good (and accepting everything he says or does) or all bad (and condemning everything he says or does).

Distorted Self-Image Those who minister to alcoholics and drug users have noticed that many of these people experience extremes in their self-concept. Sometimes they feel like Superman, able to accomplish any task and right any wrong. But at other times, they are unreasonably afraid of their own inadequacies.

Tunnel Vision People under stress sometimes can't see their options. They can only think of one solution to a problem. In Al's story, he saw drinking as his only answer. "I can't quit," he told Judy, believing he was speaking the truth. "I need alcohol to relax."

Delusional Thinking "When I drink a few beers, I'm a lot funnier, and people like me," one teenager told himself. "Doing a line makes me much more productive in the afternoon," a businessman told his buddies. "When I'm high, boys think I'm much more attractive," a girl in college believed. Some of us develop delusions that fuel our poor choices and behavior. We may not have believed these fables at first, but after a while, they become good excuses for continuing our bad choices.

Generalizations   Broad, global statements include terms such as "everybody," "nobody," always," and "never." "Everybody who is cool smokes dope" or "Nobody ever understands me" are statements which can't possibly be true and are a poor excuse for unwholesome behavior.

Perfectionism   One way we try to cope with a life and a family that is out of control is to rigidly structure them. Nobody can be a perfectionist in every area, but some of us have certain aspects of our lives—our rooms, our homework, our clothes, our appearance, or our cars—which drive us crazy if they aren't "just right." Even addicts who are hopelessly out-of-control in virtually every part of their lives may have one thing, such as the way they roll their smokes, which must be perfect. We think about that one thing endlessly, afraid we won't do it right, or someone else will mess it up.

"If it feels good . . . "   Another coping mechanism is to give up, to let go, and do whatever feels good at the time. People who are "loose and wild" may appear relaxed, but they are often full of anger at those who have made them feel out of control. They resent anyone who might question their permissive approach to life's problems.

It is almost impossible to address the problems of stinkin' thinkin' by ourselves, because we believe our thoughts are true, no matter how distorted they may be. We need outside help to become more objective. Books, tapes, CD's, and videos can help a lot if people are willing to change, but nothing can take the place of a wise friend, parent, pastor, coach, or counselor who will speak the truth in love (Eph. 4:25) to a teenager—or to adults.

Recurring thoughts are like tapes that play in our minds hour after hour, day after day. "I have to take out the old tapes and put in the new ones," one person commented. "The old tapes said things like, 'You're a bum! You'll never be anybody! Why don't you just give up?' When I realize I'm thinking those things (and that was really hard at first, but I'm getting better at it all the time), I plug in the new tapes about God's love and strength. That helps a lot!"

A NEW IDENTITY

The tapes we have allowed to play in our heads have shaped our sense of identity. To use another analogy, we get our identity from looking in the "mirrors" around us. First and foremost, our parents are mirrors that shape our self-perception when we are young. We look at them and see the message "You are a wonderful person, and I love you very much!" or "I don't have time for you." or "Can't you do anything right?! You're a failure!" or a host of other messages we internalize and believe.

In the adolescent years, our peers become important mirrors. We want to be accepted by them, and their messages reflect powerful images about us: "Hey, you're cool. We like you!" or "You're a punk! Get outta my face!" Teenagers are exceptionally sensitive to even the slightest reflection of acceptance or rejection from those whose opinions they value.

We need to replace old, negative tapes with new ones that communicate a solid identity based on the truths of Christ's love and acceptance. We also need good friends who mirror that identity. When we look in the mirror of the Scriptures, we see the grace of God on virtually every page. We don't have to be perfect or measure up in some way to earn God's love, because it isn't earned at all. It's a gift. We can relax and accept it. When we trust in Christ to be our Savior, we're saying, "I can't be good enough to make up for my sins, but Jesus did that for me on the cross."

All kinds of incredible things happen to us when we trust Christ. We are adopted into the family of God, so we can call Him Father and experience closeness to our heavenly Father even if our earthly father is distant or harsh. Because God is the King of the universe and we are His children, we are now royalty! We are forgiven and washed clean by Christ's blood. The Holy Spirit comes to dwell within us, so we actually become living temples of God!

Sometimes people ask, "Did all this happen by chance?" "Did God somehow make a mistake when He made me?" "Will He dump me if I mess up?" No, no, and no. Next question, please! The Scriptures say that God chose us to be His children. He didn't choose us because we tricked Him. He knows everything (which can be a little scary—or very comforting—when you think about it) and loves us completely. He doesn't make mistakes. Paul told the Ephesian believers that Christians have been "sealed" by the Holy Spirit in a strong relationship (Eph. 1:13).

Throughout church history, people have marvelled at the unconditional love of God and the astounding identity of being His children. Some, in fact, haven't believed it could be true. They suggested that unconditional love would be the door to more sin because we would take advantage of God's grace. Peter and Paul addressed that issue and said that the love of God is the most powerful, motivating factor in the world. Peter wrote:

But you are a chosen generation, a royal priesthood, a holy nation, His own special people, that you may proclaim the praises of Him who called you out of darkness into His marvelous light. (1 Pet. 2:9)

As we understand who we are as God's beloved children, our words and actions will show it. We will tell other people what God has done for us. Paul wrote the Corinthian believers:

For the love of Christ constrains us, because we judge thus: that if One died for all . . . that those who live should live no longer for themselves but for Him who died for them and rose again. (2 Cor. 5:14–15)

A part of our identity in Christ is that we now have a purpose—to honor Him. We will live for Him and we will make decisions about our time, money, words, behavior, and relationships that honor Him. The Bible says that Jesus came to seek and to save the lost

(Luke 19:10), and we have the privilege of doing that with Him! He wants us to join Him in fulfilling His purposes, and He has provided all the tools we need for the project: His wisdom, strength, forgiveness, and love.

Our identity is also shaped by fellow believers in our churches, schools, clubs, and Huddles. We're not talking about just sitting in the same room with someone. That doesn't do much to shape our identities. We're talking about listening to people, sharing the truth of God's Word with them, and being involved in ministry and fun together. When other believers communicate the love, wisdom, and strength of God to us, we learn to accept it and believe it. Then we are able to be good mirrors and reflect this identity to still more people.

Another factor which shapes our sense of identity is our activity. Sports, hobbies, and service give us a sense of accomplishment. We develop certain skills when we help a teenager, learn to make a good block, learn to use a router in woodworking, or see a person's life changed because we have taken the time to care. These reinforce our sense of who we are, what we are can do, and how God can use us. Thus activities, too, shape our identities.

PERSONAL RESPONSIBILITY

Irresponsibility is easy to identify in some people. We may see someone living on the streets who hasn't taken a bath in months, and who is emaciated because he's spent all his money on cocaine, and caustically say, "He's a bum!" He has allowed his need for drugs to overwhelm his sense of personal responsibility.

This is an obvious example. But many people hide their irresponsibility in certain areas of their lives by being extremely responsible in other areas. For instance, a young man may be very disciplined in his workouts and eating habits so he will be in shape, but his drive is fueled by his anger toward his controlling, manipulative mother. He won't try to talk to his mother about their relationship, and in fact, he denies there is even a problem. He is overly responsible in sports (or school or work or whatever) but irresponsible in his unwillingness to admit his hurt and take steps to resolve the problems in his relationship with his mother.

Personal responsibility includes several factors.

Self-Awareness Personal responsibility begins with self-awareness. This isn't the same thing as being self-absorbed. Self-awareness is simply an understanding of how we are affected by people and circumstances. Watch how you react to people and situations. Typically, the same people and recurring situations give us problems over and over again. When someone ridicules you, do you bark back or slink away? When someone is needy, do you try to "fix" the problem so he will appreciate you, or do you put him down as a weakling? In conflict, do you give in to get it over with, get away because you can't stand it, try to please the angry person out of fear, or use your anger to intimidate and win? Being aware of our reactions gives us the starting point—and the motivation—to change.

Watch for Signs As we become more aware of the people and situations that give us difficulties, we will be more aware of the signs that we're being propelled into wrong behaviors. Notice your clenched fist, your slumped posture, your tense shoulders, or your loud or quivery voice. Use these as triggers for the process of thinking about what you want to accomplish and how you want to accomplish it. For instance, a girl who wilts under the pressure of conflict with her father can recognize her slouched posture and quivery voice and say to herself, "Okay, this is how I normally react, but I'm going to respond differently this time. I'm going to sit up straight, look Dad in the eye, and speak the truth."

Goal-Setting Just what is this girl going to say to her father? And why and how is she going to say it? These important questions need to be answered in order to set clear goals. Her goals might be things like:

- I want to be a person instead of a punching bag for my dad.
- I want to tell him how I feel about his yelling at me.
- I want to have a good, respectful relationship with him.
- I want to have a relationship with my dad like the ones some of my friends have with theirs.
- I want to act like an adult even if my dad doesn't treat me like one.

We need to be very careful to have goals we can control. The ones we can't control are *wants*, not *goals*. Look back at the list of goals the young teen had. The first two and the last one are goals; all the others are wants. There is nothing in the world wrong with wanting those things, but we shouldn't take responsibility for decisions, feelings, and behaviors others must make and have.

Goal-setting sounds easy, but in fact, it is one of the hardest things for people who have drug or alcohol problems or people from unhealthy families to do. They need others to give insight about these goals so they can stay on track and make real progress.

Setting Boundaries   We are irresponsible when we let others make decisions for us and tell us how to feel and act. We are overly responsible when we make decisions others need to make for themselves or try to control how they feel and act. We need to set up clear boundaries of responsibilities.

- I am responsible for how I feel.
- I am responsible for how I act.
- I am responsible for my own decisions.
- I am responsible for communicating clearly and with respect.
- I am not responsible for making others happy.
- I am not responsible for other people's decisions, even if they choose to hurt themselves.

The fact that we aren't responsible for others' feelings and behavior doesn't give us license to treat them any way we choose! We are responsible before God to always treat people with respect and with kindness. The rub comes when others expect (demand) us to do more than God expects of us.

Accountability   Accountability is an important part of a teen's life. Having clear-cut boundaries can help teens keep their commitments. For instance, the One Way 2 Play—Drug Free! commitment sheet allows students to sign their names as a pledge to Christ and to each other to live and play drug free. The sheet reads:

We have accepted the challenge to strive for excellence as student athletes by choosing the One Way 2 Play—Drug Free! lifestyle!

Faith in Jesus Christ.   We believe Christ forgives us, gives us the wisdom to make good decisions, and the strength to carry them out.

Commitment to say no to alcohol and drugs.   We pledge to be strong in our commitment and to help others be strong too.

Accountability to one another.   We will regularly ask each other the hard questions:

- Are you living and playing alcohol and drug free?
- Are you encouraging others to live and play that way?
- Are you being honest with at least one mature person about your feelings and temptations?
- Are you trusting Christ to meet your needs?
- Are you honoring Him in your thoughts, words, and actions?

Using a commitment sheet can help students encourage each other and hold each other accountable. When they see a friend or teammate being tempted, they can ask him the questions on the sheet to remind him of his commitment. By being involved in each other's lives in this way we can help each other a lot!

Note: You may order a copy of the One Way 2 Play—Drug Free! commitment sheet by filling out the order form at the back of the book.

Dal

Coaches are role models. I'd like to see coaches sign the One Way 2 Play—Drug Free! commitment sheet and abstain from using drugs and alcohol. This gives them the platform to hold the team and the Huddle accountable. If a coach signs it, he can then ask the assistant coaches and players to sign it too.

I visited with a coach a couple of years ago about One Way 2 Play!, and he really got fired up about it. He then realized that if he signed the sheet, he would need to give up the beer he drank after hot, sweaty practices. He thought about it for a minute, and then said, "Dal, it's more important for me to be a good role model for my coaches and my players than it is for me to have a beer every now and then. I need to stop drinking beer anyway. This gives me a great incentive!"

We'd like coaches to take the lead in signing the commitment sheet as an example and a motivation to their teams. Then they can all hold each other accountable.

Role Plays   One of the most helpful tools in learning to communicate with difficult people is role-playing. This can be done one-on-one, but it is more helpful in a group, where people can play the roles of several family members or other people. The facilitator assigns roles, and the primary person tells how each person in his life typically acts in a given situation. He then has the opportunity to practice clear, calm, direct, respectful, honest communication in a positive environment. With his skills honed in this way, he will be better prepared to face the real event.

Grieve and Forgive   Many of us spend our lives playing elaborate games to block the pain we feel. When we are honest about this pain, we feel it deeply. When we are finally honest with others, we hope they will give us the love and attention we always wanted. Unfortunately, they usually don't. That, too, hurts deeply. What do we do with these painful emotions? We learn to grieve.

We usually associate grieving with death, but we need to realize that grieving is appropriate for all the losses we experience. The death of our hope of being loved by a parent, a girlfriend, a boyfriend, a brother, or a sister is excruciating. We need to grieve over the loss.

The realization of loss is also a realization of an offense that needs to be forgiven. As long as we deny the reality of the offense, we are denying the need to forgive. Unforgiveness festers and becomes bitterness, clouding every relationship (even though we may be unaware of the real cause or effects).

Forgiveness requires two things: a genuine grasp of the offense and a genuine grasp of Christ's forgiveness of us. Both of these may take time, but we need to forgive as much as we can as soon as we can. Paul encouraged the Ephesian believers to "be kind to one another, tenderhearted, forgiving one another, just as God in Christ also forgave you" (Eph. 4:32).

WHAT DO YOU DO WHEN ♦ ♦ ♦ ?

When it comes to drinking and drugging, the crucial, decision-making point occurs when someone puts the squeeze on a person to start or use again. The pressure may look like an invitation at first, but progressively, the heat is turned up.

Young people must learn to respond to temptations from peers calmly and with a sense of confidence. Help them anticipate who will tempt them and how they'll do it. Encourage them to talk to a friend about it, and help them practice their responses. They need to be ready.

The first line of response is to ignore the pressure completely or change the subject. An old buddy says, "Hey, I got some weed over here with your name on it. It's usually three dollars a hit, but for you, it's free. Hey, you can't beat that, my man!"

How should someone respond? He could just walk by, but the manipulator may not settle for that. Actually, the best response may be not to respond at all. Instead, he can change the subject. "Hey, you made a C on that math quiz, didn't you? Did you get the answer to the last questions? I missed it. How did you work it out?"

If the manipulator ignores attempts to change the subject and persists in applying pressure, the teenager can say, "Thanks, but I'm not interested." If he is clear and confident in his response, people usually get the message sooner or later (although it may take a while).

Some other responses include:

- If I use that stuff, I might get grounded and lose my driver's license for three months. It's not worth it.
- You know, I really don't like that stuff.
- I appreciate the offer. That's not for me.
- Thanks, but I've thought about it, and I decided not to.

People who pressure us either feel insecure about their own use of alcohol or drugs and want us to participate to validate their own behavior, or they are trying to sell us some dope so they can make some money. The point is: They aren't looking out for us. We have to look out for ourselves. If they sense we are nervous or unsure how to respond, they are like hungry hyenas on a crippled antelope. They move in for the kill!

Encourage young people to be ready, especially if they are longtime users trying to quit. Teach them to be confident in their response, even if they don't feel confident. Tell them what the deodorant commercial used to say: "Never let 'em see you sweat!"

DEVELOPING HEALTHY HABITS

It takes dedication and discipline to be a good athlete, and it takes at least as much dedication and discipline to change the habits of a lifetime. Someone once observed that it takes seven times longer to unlearn a bad habit and learn a new good one than it would have taken to learn the good new one in the beginning. But some of us don't have the luxury of starting at the beginning. We have to start where we are. Today. Right now.

Habits are built a day at a time, and even a moment at a time. A hundred times a day, we choose to do things the old way or a new way. We may be motivated by any number of things: we want to get over being depressed; we are tired of hurting others; we don't want to act like our parents; a girlfriend said she would leave us if we didn't change; or we want to experience God's love and grace. When we are motivated, we set goals. These goals need to be realistic and attainable. If they are too high and grandiose, we'll probably fail and quit trying.

A friend, coach, pastor, or counselor can help young people (and parents and coaches) set goals and then hold them accountable for meeting them. They may be everyday types of goals, such as being on time for school or work, doing homework, taking care of specific responsibilities, and getting to sleep by 11:30 every night. Or they may be goals to communicate with family members, return something stolen, or avoid certain people who are bad influences.

Sometimes we try to get as close as we can to the line without crossing it. That's a dangerous game when it comes to drugs and alcohol, because it can cost us our relationships, our reputation, and our future. Don't mess around! Stay as far away from temptations as you can. Paul was well aware of this temptation to get close to the line. He warned the Romans:

Let us walk properly, as in the day, not in revelry and drunkenness, not in licentiousness and lewdness, not in strife and envy. But put on the Lord Jesus Christ, and make no provision for the flesh, to fulfill its lusts. (Rom. 13:13–14)

Paul said to not even think about giving in to sinful desires, but instead, to wrap God's truth, God's Spirit, and God's people around you to encourage and protect you. That was good advice to the Romans 1,900 years ago. It's good advice for you and me today.

But there's only been one perfect person, so we can be sure that we will blow it from time to time. The farther we get from dangerous behavior, however, the less damaging our mess-ups will be. For instance, getting to bed a little late one night is not nearly as harmful as going out partying with our pot-smoking friends. Set realistic goals, and give yourself some room to grow and change. Don't expect perfection. Most important, be careful not to put yourself in tempting situations where you have slipped often in the past. That's asking for trouble!

After all is said and done, the growth process isn't a mystery at all. It's hard work. It calls for setting boundaries and goals in behavior, finding Christian friends who will encourage you, and being prepared for every situation. Coupled with the work of God's Spirit in your heart, you will find new identity, strong motivation, and real hope. Change is difficult. It takes heart, discipline, good teammates, and a great coach. You've got that!

8

THE POWER OF THE HUDDLE

In Jenks, Oklahoma, the high school Fellowship of Christian Athletes Huddle had an answer to alcohol-related violence at the school. Helped by Bob Smith, coach and Huddle leader, the members formulated a plan that included student and parent contracts stipulating abstinence from any and all drug use during the school year. Dr. Gene Buinger, superintendent at Jenks, approved the concept but wanted to expand it beyond athletics to include band, drama, cheerleading, and other activities. He also wanted to apply the program from the sixth through the twelfth grades.

Caring Parents, a local organization, provided encouragement to the students. At a school-wide meeting, over a thousand students and parents met with school officials as well as police and hospital representatives. The program, which included the provision that no high school students would be permitted to participate in extracurricular activities unless they signed the contract to abstain from alcohol and drugs during the school year, was approved. Parents signed a similar contract promising to monitor the students' compliance.

Consequences for breaking the contract are stiff. The first offense brings a suspension from activities for ten days, though the student can continue to practice with the team. The second offense brings an eighteen-week suspension—with no practice privileges. However, if the student obtains counseling from a licensed professional counselor, he or she can be reinstated after two weeks.

The program is based on the honor system. "If the student says he didn't drink or use drugs, we believe him," Smith says.

Students claim the program works. Though there have been some who abuse the system, most students have been honest and committed to their pledge. The culture of the students has been positively affected. One example of this change is that alcohol is no longer permitted at after-school events.

Another positive result of this program is that the Fellowship of Christian Athletes Huddle grew rapidly. Attendance doubled in the first year. "The kids are coming because we are giving them the kind of activities they want," Smith says. "They were screaming for this, but no one heard them. They have emotional and spiritual needs. We brought them together and gave them an alternative lifestyle. We aren't dragging them. They come because they want to. What we've done is take the good kids in our school and kept them going in the right direction. By joining, students are saying, 'We will make a difference in our high school.' They just decided somebody had to do something now to change this thing. You can't wait until you're a professional athlete to change. It starts right here, and they did it. A lot of the school personnel laughed. A lot of them didn't want this, but when they saw how the students were behind it, they changed their minds. It's working. The students are making it work. They are making a difference."[1]

We have all heard stories of people who said, "My coach (or my youth pastor) believed in me when I didn't believe in myself. I don't know what my life would have been like without him (or her)." Coaches and youth leaders have the incredible opportunity to nurture young lives. For many of these young people, the Huddle or youth group is their last and best hope of finding real love and strength.

The way we build a family environment in our groups is by treating people like honored family members—with love, honesty, and respect. Be honest with the Lord and yourself about your own hurts, fears, anger, hopes, and dreams. These are universal emotions; no one escapes them. As you are honest about your own feelings, you will be more genuine with others in the group.

Honesty is a vital ingredient in a healthy family. However, don't take it too far. Be wise about sharing too much detail about your problems, and don't tell about somebody else's struggles unless you can mask the person's identity. People are attracted to leaders who can admit they are human and struggle with life's problems. If the parents in a family, the coach in a Huddle, or the leader of the youth group model this vulnerability, others will be far more likely to be honest about their own problems.

Commitments are important in families. The Scriptures are filled with encouragement about the quality of our relationships. We are to love one another, accept one another, encourage one another, forgive one another, admonish one another, and honor one another. We are also told to commit ourselves to one another and to demonstrate our commitment in tangible and intangible ways.

We can also commit to avoid sarcastic comments which get some laughs at the expense of the victims of our "humor." Coaches, group leaders, and all of us need to model positive, affirming language. We need to talk about the power of the tongue fairly often and the damage it can inflict or blessings it can bestow.

A loving, strong, family atmosphere creates positive peer pressure among the Huddle or group members. Instead of pressuring each other to participate in destructive behaviors, they will put the squeeze on each other to do what is good and right.

Dal

Peer pressure can have a very powerful and positive effect on us. I remember when we finished boot camp in the Marine Corps, we had a big, blowout celebration. Like everybody else, I had worked really hard at becoming a Marine, and I wanted to enjoy this party.

I'll never forget getting a can of beer and sitting down at a table with my drill instructor. He looked at me and said, "Shealy, what are you doing with that beer?"

"I'm going to drink it to celebrate my graduation like everybody else," I replied.

The sergeant knew I didn't drink. He looked at me real hard and told me, "Shealy, you don't have to drink beer to be a Marine."

I really respected this man. He was a war veteran. He was a senior drill instructor. He was a rough, tough Marine. But he told me that drinking didn't make me a better Marine. I put the beer down.

I'm not the kind of person to do anything halfway. If I had started drinking, I'm afraid it would have ruined my life. My parents had a strong, positive influence on me. My drill instructor and coaches like Gus Allen, Roy Harmon, and Frosty Holt also shaped my life, and I am deeply grateful to each of them. I've seen several of my football players destroy their lives and careers by using alcohol and drugs. One high school classmate literally drank himself to death. Another young man had everything in the world going for him, but his career went down the drain because he chose drinking over self-control. Some of my friends and some coaches I know have gotten off the path and made some bad choices in regard to drinking and living wild. It's a tempting lifestyle, and it would have been very easy for me to have gone down that road if I hadn't gotten the encouragement and accountability of my parents and coaches.

An emotionally healthy family, group, or Huddle is a safe place, a place where people are respected. Confidentiality on the part of the leader is an important part of that respect. If young people know they can talk openly without being corrected, condemned, or challenged, they will probably be open to your help. Confidentiality, however, is a difficult issue in working with adolescents, because you sometimes learn facts that must be communicated to authorities. For instance, if a girl tells you she is being sexually molested by her father or another family member, you are required by law to report that to Child Protective Services. Don't let this keep you from being a person young people feel safe talking to. When you explain that you want the group to be a place where they feel loved and safe, you can also tell them that you are required to report physical or sexual abuse to the authorities. Have some referral sources available for those who need help. Take some time to evaluate the philosophy and effectiveness of these professionals so you can have confidence when you send someone to see them.

If they have nowhere to go, many young people hang out at malls, in unsupervised homes, or other places where they are likely to get into trouble. The Huddle or youth group provides a wholesome alternative. Many churches have excellent youth programs that are open to non-members. An assistant coach can plan meetings or events that are stimulating and encouraging for adolescents, especially those at risk.

Here are some *do*s and *don't*s to consider when attempting to help teens who are hurting, drinking, or using drugs.

- Don't confront the person when he or she is high.
- Don't yell, overreact, lecture, or preach.
- Don't let him blame you for his behavior and its consequences. Don't blame yourself either.
- Don't accept excuses such as "Everybody's doing it!"
- Don't command him to do anything. Tell him what *you* are going to do.
- Don't make empty threats. Do what you say you will do.
- Do be calm.
- Do communicate that you care and that that's why you are getting involved.
- Do be objective. Don't exaggerate or deny the reality of the situation.
- Do plan ahead. Know what you are going to do so that you can state it clearly and firmly.
- Do use the accountability sign to remind him to live and play drug free.

- Do get help. Contact someone who specializes in chemical dependency and codependency counseling.[2]

Many young people have nowhere to go for love and respect. Their families don't provide the affirmation and stability they need, so they go to their friends. But their friends are just as lonely, angry, and hurt as they are, so they only "pool their ignorance" with those who can identify with them. As a coach, youth leader, or parent, you can provide a nurturing atmosphere where young people learn to grieve their hurts, forgive their offenders, and learn new coping skills.

9

THE COACH'S CORNER

Dal

One year when I was a coach at Richmond, our team lost a heart-breaking game to a team we should have beaten. That night, Barbara and I went out to eat, and at the restaurant, we saw one of our star players with his girlfriend and his parents. We exchanged some pleasant conversation about how we had to get back on track the next week, and then Barbara and I were seated at a table across the room.

A few hours later, at about 2:00 A.M., I was awakened by a call from the campus police. They had arrested this star player for drunk driving on campus, and they wanted to know if I would come to the station. It seems he had a fight with his girlfriend after they had taken his parents back to their hotel room. He then got drunk and drove like a wild man on the campus streets. I had a heart-to-heart talk with this young man, and I suspended him for one game.

Later that week, someone told me that another starter on our team had been seen buying beer at a store. I called the young man into my office and asked him to tell me the truth. He stammered a little, but he admitted he had bought the beer. He said, "But, Coach, I didn't get drunk or anything!" I told him that didn't matter. Buying *and drinking beer was a violation of the team rules. I suspended him for one game too.*

The next Saturday, we entered the game without two key players who had made dumb decisions. Their absence from the field hurt us. All day, we struggled on the field. We were just a little out of sync. We lost a very close game.

I walked into the locker room and closed the door. The boys didn't have to guess that I was upset. I challenged them: "Men, I want men who are willing to put the team first and who are men enough to have self-control. We may not have many who are willing to do that, but if I only have eleven who will, that's the team we'll have! Right now, I want to challenge each one of you to look inside and see what you want, if you want to be on this team, and if you're willing to put the team first so that you don't hurt the team by making dumb decisions." (Our team was called the Richmond Spiders, and to state our team spirit, people said, "I'm in the web.") I told them, "If you want to be on this team, I want you to come up, look me in the eye, shake my hand, and tell me, 'Coach, I'm in the web!'"

Every boy came up to me. They all pledged to put the team first. The rest of the story, as Paul Harvey might say, is that we won our next six ball games, and we won our conference championship on national television.

Coaches have to be examples for their teams, and they'd better enforce their own rules. It cost us a game to suspend those two players, but the experience taught us a lesson about teamwork and making a commitment to something much higher than an emotional release or a cold drink.

Many anti-drug campaigns have been implemented to help young people say no to drugs. These campaigns raise the awareness of the problem, but they seldom address its root causes. Telling people to stop a behavior usually isn't effective if you have not dealt with the forces that drove the person to that behavior. One Way 2 Play—Drug Free! addresses the forces in young people's lives that create the stress, hurt, and anger they are trying to alleviate with alcohol or drugs. When these root causes are addressed, teenagers can respond appropriately and develop new skills in decision making and living.

ADDRESS ROOT CAUSES

This may seem like the easiest step in the process, but it is usually the most difficult. Every emotional and relational dynamic in the family is designed to block pain. Addressing the causes of the pain is paddling upstream against every inclination. Family members have avoided dealing with these issues because they lurked like hideous monsters, ready to mangle anyone who awakened them. It sometimes seems better to just leave them alone.

But people can't experience healing if they won't let the doctor examine the wound. As they talk about their hopes and fears, as they laugh and cry, young people realize that they can be honest about their own pain. And as we teach them about the powerful forces of emotional pain and anger, and the roles they play to deal with these feelings, they will feel understood. They will learn to identify the stresses, negative feelings, and destructive behaviors in their lives too.

Some adolescents will understand immediately and be ready to get the help they need. Perhaps they are at the end of their rope and are desperate for help. Others will take longer to comprehend what you are saying. Be patient with them. They aren't stupid. It's just that they feel so threatened by their own monsters of pain and anger that they need time to develop the courage to face them. Some never do. No matter how eloquently you speak, some people never catch on. Even the most skilled counselors can't predict who will take a long time to share and who will never catch on. So don't give up! It may be years later that the person desperately needs help and remembers, "My coach once told me that the problem isn't the booze; it's the pain that the booze numbs. I need to deal with that pain."

In One Way 2 Play—Drug Free!, we focus on the underlying

causes of stress and pain, not just the behavior they produce. Everyone (not just the alcohol and drug abusers) experiences pain to some degree, so this program ministers to everyone. It is also universally applicable because it meets universal needs.

- If a teen has never taken a drink, this program gives her information on alcohol and drugs and lets her make a commitment to avoid them.
- If a teen is a recreational user, it warns him of the dangers he faces and gives him an opportunity and the accountability he needs to stop.
- If a teen is in a more advanced stage of abuse or addiction, it gives him a place to admit his dependency and face the pain he is trying to escape. It also offers him additional resources—like referral to a school counselor or some other source—and the encouragement and accountability to stay clean and sober.

TEACH SKILLS

Changing habits is difficult even under the best of circumstances, but new coping skills are necessary for people who don't know how to handle stress appropriately. Huddle coaches and group leaders don't need a Ph.D. to teach these skills; they are commonsense solutions to fundamental human problems. There are three skills every person needs to learn: to identify feelings and pressures, to set goals, and to take appropriate action. Let's examine them.

Identify feelings and pressures. One of the primary characteristics of a person from a dysfunctional family is a lack of objectivity. Everyone around a young woman clearly sees the devastating effects of her father's alcoholism (or her parents' divorce or any of a myriad of family stresses), and they see how she is trying to cope with the feelings of hurt and abandonment by sleeping around. But she doesn't see the connection at all. "Hey, it's fun and it doesn't hurt anybody!" she exclaims defensively.

A young man who once made good grades, practiced hard at basketball, and had lots of friends experiences the pain of his father's death. In only a few months, he drops out of sports, is failing several subjects, and has a new set of friends—the druggies. When his mother tries to talk to him, he retorts angrily, "Dad always told me to make my own decisions, and that's what I'm doing! Get off my back!"

A young man from a strict, religious home lives with a nagging, overwhelming sense of guilt and shame because he can't measure up to his parents' lofty expectations of perfection. From the outside, he is the picture of a fine Christian boy, but his anger, hurt, and shame are eating him alive. He doesn't see that the expectations are unrealistic, and he believes, "I *have to* live up to God's [actually his parents'] standards, and sometimes I don't even want to. I must be a *really* bad person!" He feels alone, ashamed, and confused.

You can help people identify their feelings and the stressful situations that cause them by doing the following.

- Model the ability to identify feelings as you tell your own stories, "I felt angry (or hurt or ashamed or sad or . . .) when I . . . "
- Talk about feelings as you give examples of contemporary stories or biblical characters. For example, "Peter wept bitterly after he denied Jesus."
- Put yourself or others in the stories. "Imagine how you would have felt if you had been Peter. You had just let down the man you said you would die for."
- Ask for feedback. Ask, "How would you have felt if you had been Peter?" Let group or team members answer without correcting or criticizing any responses. (Different people may feel different emotions about the same event.)
- Give them "emotion options" to help them identify their feelings. It isn't uncommon for people to be emotionally frozen if they have experienced severe trauma. They may need help. Ask gently, "Did you feel hurt? Sad? Angry? Afraid? Ashamed?" In doing so, you're giving them a vocabulary to express their feelings when they learn to identify them.

- Validate their feelings by validating the significance of their stresses. Say something like "When parents split up, that shakes up your *whole world*! You don't know who you can count on anymore! No wonder you feel so hurt and angry!"
- Remember that for wounded people, even small stresses produce pain. Don't tell someone, "You shouldn't feel that way!" Instead, look for the deeper wound which beneath the present pain. Say, "That hurt you a lot. I wonder if there are bigger hurts making this one seem worse."

It is crucial to identify feelings and stresses, but that's just the first step. When the problem is identified, we can help them set goals to overcome the problem.

Set goals. We talk a lot about setting goals in sports, but few of us know how to set them in the most crucial areas of our lives: our behaviors and relationships. Adolescents have difficulty in this area, because they are trying to figure out what it means to be a responsible adult. The transition from childhood (when others set goals for you) to adulthood (when you set your own goals and are responsible for your own behavior) is a rite of passage in life. You can help the people in your Huddle or group by explaining and reinforcing two simple but life-changing principles.

First, ask questions. "What are you responsible for? And what are you *not* responsible for?" People are responsible for their own behavior, their own choices, and their own responses to problems. We aren't responsible for other people's behavior, choices, and responses. Many of us get confused about this issue. We believe other people are responsible for our happiness, health, wealth, and comfort, and we get very angry when these expectations aren't met. And strangely, many of us feel it is our responsibility to make other people happy, healthy, wealthy, and comfortable.

Many of us expect someone else to protect us from the consequences of our behavior. For instance, a boy doesn't study, but he expects his father's position as a respected local businessman to ward off problems with his teachers.

Dal

Some coaches have the attitude: "I don't care what you do on your own time as long as you perform." These coaches don't discipline anyone for anything unless they are forced to take steps by the athletic director or the news media.

Other coaches use drills to discipline players. If a player is caught driving under the influence, the coach may get him out at six o'clock the next morning for sprints or grass drills. In this way, some coaches try to show that wrong behaviors will have painful consequences.

Many coaches suspend players for a game or two depending on the severity of the offense. After a second or third offense, the player may be permanently suspended. A few coaches have policies that automatically and permanently dismiss a player from a team if the player is involved in using street drugs, because using is a felony offense. Usually, the player is then sent to some kind of treatment program, but since the coach no longer has any clout with the player, he usually doesn't go to treatment.

Sadly, some coaches have open bars for their players at banquets at the end of the year. Coaches need to understand that what they condone and what they permit has an effect on players. They need to model self-control and maturity, and they need to provide an environment that promotes self-control and maturity.

Our high school football program hadn't had a winning season for ten or eleven years when I joined the team. That year, we got a new coach, Gus Allen, who tried to instill in us a winning attitude. He was my coach for football, basketball, and baseball, and I also had him for two classes in school. In all, I had about six hours of personal contact with him each day, and he became something of a father figure to me.

During the summer, he picked me up at five o'clock in the morning, and we worked in the peach orchards or in the peach packing plant. Sometimes we wouldn't get home until midnight or one in the morning, and we went back to work at five the next morning.

Coach Allen had a great deal of influence on me, and I'm very thankful to him. He was the kind of guy who would drive you and push you to be your very best. He was interested in all aspects of our lives. If our grades dropped for any reason, he would really chew us out, and sometimes he even used "the board of education"! During my senior year, he took me around to visit different colleges to see about playing football for them. My parents couldn't afford to send me to school, and it was my high school coach who encouraged me to excel in school and athletics, and he helped me get a scholarship to college.

My college coach, Roy Harmon, had a very different style, but he had a profound influence on me also. He was a very strong Christian and a low-key person. I had been a churchgoer, but I didn't know much about having a personal relationship with the Lord. As I watched his life and listened to him, I made a commitment to Christ. After that, he took me with him to speak to civic clubs and churches, and in fact, he taught me how to share my faith in Christ. After being with him for four years, I decided I wanted to be a coach like him.

Second, explore the options. We get stuck in a rut. We respond the same way to the same circumstances simply because we've always responded that way. We need to consider the full range of options and choose the one that is best. For example, a girl who's dating a guy with a drinking problem has a number of options. She can:

- keep dating him without addressing the issue
- stop dating him without telling him why
- ask a friend to tell him to stop drinking
- demand that he prove his love for her by stopping his drinking
- talk to a school counselor about how to handle the situation
- tell him she prefers that he not drink so much, and if he continues, she will stop dating him

- tell him she cares for him and sees how he's messing up his life by drinking
- tell him that she doesn't think it's good to date anymore until his drinking is under control

Obviously, some of these are good options and some aren't. The object is to find the best choices among the possiblities. One way to determine the best choice is to analyze the possible or probable consequences of each action. Here are some principles to help us.

Know your usual pattern of responses. We are creatures of habit. If we realize how we normally react or respond in certain situations, we will be prepared to make necessary changes. Some of us withdraw; we need to be more assertive. Some of us attack; we need to calm down and listen. Some of us use self-pity to manipulate others; we need to be honest and responsible. The following pair of questions will clarify our position.

1. How do I usually feel and act in situations like this?
2. How do I need to act this time?

Be realistic. It is counterproductive and self-defeating to set unrealistic goals. A student with a D average probably shouldn't set a goal of straight A's. That may not be attainable. All C's would be better. If he makes that, he can go for B's the next term. Similarly, a girl who is abusing tranquilizers is unrealistic to think she can just quit and be all right. Something drove her to use the drug, and using it didn't solve the underlying problem. In fact, it probably made the problem worse. A more realistic goal is to see a counselor to resolve the stresses that led to drug use in the first place.

Be specific. One of the most common problems in goal-setting is that we tend to be vague and global. For example, we say, "I want to be happy." Happiness may be a worthwhile goal, but it is often a result of achieving other goals. We can set identifiable goals for even the smallest of events, and in fact, these "small events" are the building blocks that determine the shape of our lives.

Leaders, coaches, and group members can learn to ask themselves questions such as, "What do I want in this relationship?"

"What do I need to communicate in this conversation?" "What am I trying to accomplish by acting this way?" "What is my goal in making this decision?" and "What is my goal in life?"

Take action. When clear goals have been set, it's time for action. Several principles help us take important steps toward accomplishing our goals.

Get help. Wisdom requires that we solicit mature guidance all along the path that leads toward our goal, particularly as we set out to refine our plan. We also need someone to encourage us and hold us accountable.

Resolve the underlying problems. Part of taking appropriate action is to grieve and forgive. Others have hurt us. They have offended us. We experienced a deep sense of loss because of their neglect, ridicule, abuse, manipulation, or abandonment. The appropriate response is to grieve, to feel sadness about how we have been treated, and to forgive those who have hurt us. This forgiveness may not come easily because it is based on progressive understanding of our hurts. But it is also based on our own experience of Christ's forgiveness of us.

The entire message of One Way 2 Play—Drug Free! could be capsulized in three actions: *grieve*, *forgive*, and *take responsibility*. These words are the heart of the program.

Seek positive environments. Many of us want to change, but we remain riveted in the same lifestyle and relationships that reinforce the old, destructive behaviors. Some religious leaders take the easy route by demanding compliance to a set of legalistic standards. They say, "If you listen to anything but Christian music or read anything but Christian books, you're going to fall!" Others go even farther: "If you listen to anything but hymns, you're falling into the devil's trap! Christian rock music is from Satan!"

Music, books, videos, movies, and friends all influence our lives. Coaches and group leaders need to address these important topics reasonably. Paul wrote, "All things are lawful for me, but all things are not helpful. All things are lawful for me, but I will not be brought under the power of any" (1 Cor 6:12). Help teens see that they can make their own decisions about these things, and that they will also experience the consequences, either good or bad. Some will listen and some won't. But your example and encouragement will make a great difference.

Prepare for reactions. People who attempt something new and threatening experience the thrill of victory or the agony of defeat. They are vulnerable to tremendous highs and lows, and these emotional swings are accentuated by the volatility of adolescence. As you talk with the group or individuals about significant steps in their lives, prepare them for possible reactions after they take the steps by explaining, "You may feel . . . or you may feel . . . And you'll be tempted to go back to the way you've responded before if you think you've failed. Or you may think you'll never have a problem in this area again if you succeed. Be careful. Be realistic."

Be strong! The Lord must know how difficult it is to do something new because the Scriptures are full of admonitions to be strong and courageous. The unknown frightens us. Even a stouthearted, proven man like Joshua needed the Lord's encouragement: "Have I not commanded you? Be strong and of good courage; do not be afraid, nor be dismayed, for the LORD your God is with you wherever you go" (Josh. 1:9).

No matter how carefully we've planned and prepared, most of us get jelly-legged and mush-brained when it's time to speak the truth to someone or change a behavior for the first time. We need to be reminded to hang in there!

One Way 2 Play—Drug Free! isn't just a one-shot program. It is designed to help you create a permanently positive environment with a family atmosphere. In the future, we plan to provide a series of One Way 2 Play! materials which focus on the problems and opportunities young people face every day. These topics will be relevant, biblical, and application-oriented.

We realize that some coaches and group leaders will be able to implement these concepts naturally and easily; others will have more difficulty. That's okay. We know you care for these young people or you wouldn't be leading them in the first place. Be patient with yourself as you try new ways of dealing with these difficult issues, and ask for help whenever you need it.

The problems we address in this program are not solved easily. Studies show that the best solution is a concerted effort involving groups, school counselors, professional counselors and agencies, and parents. As you address these issues, some young people will need more help than the group can provide, so do some homework and locate helpful resources in your community. Most have competent, qualified Christian counselors who can provide assistance, but take the extra step and call a pastor or two to find out if these counselors use the Scriptures and talk about God's love, forgiveness, and strength. When you find those who combine clinical expertise with Christian principles, you can feel confident about referring people to them.

Your responsibilities as a coach or group leader may not automatically extend to ministering to parents, but perhaps you can be a catalyst in helping a church or other organization provide information, encouragement, and help for them. Just as young people need to grieve, forgive, and take responsibility, parents do too. And if both parents and children seek the Lord and let Him work in their lives, the entire family can be changed.

At this point, you may feel overwhelmed. We want to help you accomplish your goal of helping young people follow Christ and make good choices with their lives. We recognize, however, that this program requires new skills for many Huddle coaches and youth leaders. Therefore, we recommend that you recruit an assistant coach or leader (or two!) to help you with various aspects of this program. The assistants may have abilities that complement your own, and as a team, you can meet far more needs than you could meet alone.

To help you implement this program, we're providing:

- a Group Leader's Guide (Appendix B), which includes plans for two meetings; a copy of the One Way 2 Play—Drug Free! commitment sheet, which you can ask group or team members

to sign as a pledge to live and play drug-free; and a "Group Dynamics" section to help you lead your team, Huddle, or group
- crisis counseling information (Appendix C)
- an order form for more commitments sheets, as well as our colorful One Way 2 Play—Drug Free! T-shirts, patches, and bumper stickers to reinforce the commitment to live honorably and sensibly for Christ (also good conversation starters)

We're excited about One Way 2 Play—Drug Free! and we believe God will use it—and you—to change lives! If you have any questions, please call your local Fellowship of Christian Athletes staff member or call our national office at 816-289-0909.

Grant Teaff

Former head coach at Baylor University; executive director of the American Football Coaches Association

Every coach I know can tell horror stories about kids and drugs. That's why many of us are driven to do anything we can to turn this country back to sound values. I've seen youngsters lose their scholarships, give up great opportunities, and go down the tube because of poor decisions about drugs. I had one player who was an All-American and a first-round draft choice . He had everything in the world, but after being in the pros for a few years, he got involved in drugs and his life is virtually destroyed. Last time I heard from him, he was in jail. Here was a young man who had everything, but he let drugs completely destroy his faith, his family, his fortune, and his future.

And nobody saw it coming.

I've seen many other instances of young people who got started

in drugs, but by early detection, their lives were changed. In college athletics, we have an excellent drug testing system. It not only is a deterrent, it provides early detection so we can clamp down on someone in a New York minute. We also have excellent counselors who can help young people see the truth and make better decisions. Early detection, counseling, and a good athletic policy has changed a lot of lives. That's one reason I'm excited about One Way 2 Play! It provides the best opportunity to get people the help they need as early as possible.

Coaches, parents, and teachers recognize that young people are under tremendous pressure, and youngsters need all the tools they can get. One Way 2 Play! is a terrific way to reach these young people! The key is implementation. Young people need knowledge and understanding, but most of what they get is in a negative vein. We need to do everything in our power to give them positive information that they can "sink their teeth into" so they can make real progress in their personal lives.

Its not just enough to tell somebody you need to say no. They need more than that. We need to give them good role models and teach them how to set goals and make good choices about their behaviors and relationships. Of course the ultimate difference-maker is Jesus Christ. Young people need to understand that Christ can make a tremendous difference in their lives. As Paul wrote in Romans 12:1–2, when your mind is remade, your whole nature can be transformed. Then you can begin to understand God's purpose and plan for your life. God wants us to experience His love and strength, but God gave each of us responsibility to make decisions each day to live the way He wants us to live. We have to go back to the basics of Christ's death to pay for our sins and His strength to help us live for him. Through Him, we can reach goals we never dreamed of reaching. He wants the very best for us.

One Way 2 Play! helps us "get high on life," and young people can experience the joys of setting and achieving goals each day. But many of them have never experienced that joy. One Way 2 Play!

gives us tools to help young people set a good course for their lives . . . and stay on that course.

I wish coaches would understand the tremendous influence they have on young people and their entire community. Whether they believe it or not, they are highly respected. I would like to see coaches take a public stand and embrace the One Way 2 Play! program because it is a designed plan that is really effective. It has a chance to help us solve this horrendous problem we have in this country.

10

PARENTS, FOR EXAMPLE

Note: The principles in this chapter are designed for parents, but coaches, group leaders, and group members can learn from them too.

Jay Barker
University of Alabama quarterback

I've never had a drink of alcohol, and I've never taken any drugs. I can honestly say that I've never even been tempted to get involved in drinking or drugs because it just wasn't attractive to me. I never saw it in my home, so I wasn't accustomed to it. Also, as a Christian I realized that drinking and using drugs just isn't right. My testimony is very important to me, and drinking would hinder my ability to honor Him.

My mom and my dad have been a great example to me. They are strong Christians, and they led Bible studies the whole time I was growing up. In fact, they led Bible studies with high school and college kids, so I was exposed to some really strong young people who lived for Christ. Some people hear me talk about my family, and they say, "But that's not reality." But it is reality. It's God's reality of how a home should be and how our lives should be lived. When I got out into the world, I had been grounded in Scripture, so I had a foundation to make good decisions in life.

My parents' lives were (and are) very attractive to me. They are honest. They admit they aren't perfect and that they are sinners. The biggest thing is: what they taught, they lived. They didn't just tell me what to do. They modeled it. My father is a man of God with tremendous compassion. He showed love to my sister and me by hugging us and letting us realize we were special to him. A lot of times, fathers try to have a "macho" image, so they don't want to hug their kids. But it's never been that way with us. We still hug each other. That's meant a lot to me. Sometimes men think that hugging will make their kids weak, but my dad's hugs made me stronger. It made me realize that men can love one another and show our compassion. My dad's example will help me as a father to love my kids. Little boys need their father's love, not just a cold shoulder and demands to straighten up. My dad was always open to me. We went fishing on Saturdays, and we talked about everything you could think about! I really appreciate the time he spent with me. A kid spells love: T-I-M-E, and that's what my dad gave me. And my mom was always there for me too.

Through studying God's Word, God gives us the perfect game plan for our lives. In John 10:10, Jesus says, "I came that they might have life and that they may have it more abundantly." So God gives us much more than the ability to say no to drugs. He also gives us real meaning and purpose. His guidelines aren't meant to spoil all our fun. He wants us to have even more fun than anything this world offers. He lets us know that there are consequences for sins like drinking and drugs. Often, the painful things we experience aren't God's punishment. They are just the natural consequences of our own choices. It's like God says to us, "Look, you're creating the pain on your own. I'm trying to tell you how to live so you will have peace, success, and an abundant life." I think sometimes God thinks, "These guys are just crazy! They don't want to listen to me, and I'm the One who created them!" God knows us best. He knows what we need, and His guidelines are meant to give us both protection and purpose.

Here at college, I'm in Bible studies with some other guys, I have a Christian roommate, and I have some good friends who are really strong believers. All this gives me accountability. If I step out of line even a little bit, they're going to let me know it! And if they step out of line, I'm going to let them know it. We watch out for each other all the time. Some people want to destroy Christian athletes. They spread all kinds of crazy rumors to hurt us, and we need the accountability and encouragement of good Christian friends to help us. The Lord never meant for us to be Lone Rangers. He wants us to be there for each other to encourage each other. As Hebrews 10:25 says, ". . . not forsaking the assembling of ourselves together, as is the manner of some, but exhorting one another, and so much the more as you see the Day approaching." That's what we try to do: spur one another along to continually grow in Christ.

I'm glad I didn't get involved in drinking and drugs because I could have become an alcoholic (there's alcoholism in our family history) and because I wouldn't be able to be the athlete I want to be. But the number one reason is that my testimony for Christ wouldn't be as strong. I'm not saying that somebody who has used alcohol or drugs can't have a strong testimony, but in today's society, kids need to know they can get through this life without drugs and drinking. We don't need drugs. Christ can give us all the fun and excitement we can handle!

Young people who don't know Christ are going to struggle because only Christ can give us the power to overcome. These kids need to trust Christ to become their Lord and Savior. Christian kids need to be grounded in Scripture so they can let the Word guide them in every area of life: drinking, sex, and everything else. Life isn't easy, but God gives us the Scriptures to help us fight the temptations we face.

Also, we need each other. We can stay strong if we stay together. I had some good Christian friends in high school, and we decided early on that we weren't going to drink. We didn't need it. Later I realized that people looked up to me more because I didn't drink than they would have if I had gone along with the crowd.

When I was first approached about drinking in the seventh grade, it was hard to say no that very first time. Everybody kidded me, "Why not? Why not?" I continued to say no. Real soon, people came up to me and said, "We know you don't want to drink, and that's cool. No problem. That's who you are, and that's okay." I thought, "Hey Lord, you're covering for me! I said no and now you're making that a really good thing!" Even though it was hard at first, it's a discipline. The Bible talks about discipline being hard at first. It hurts. It's painful, but after a while, it becomes a joy to us, and God blesses us because of the discipline in our lives. I saw that in my experience. When I said no at first, people ragged on me, but when I stayed strong, God blessed me. These same people looked at me and asked, "What makes you different?"

The greatest compliment I ever got was in high school when some friends said to me, "Jay, I wish I was like you. I wish I'd never started drinking." They remembered a camp-out in the mountains when we were twelve years old. My parents wouldn't let me go. (I guess they somehow knew what would happen.) That night was when these friends first started drinking and smoking pot. God really protected me when my parents didn't let me go. These friends said they wished they had never started because they really struggle with it.

Kids who aren't believers need the Lord. That's the only way they can develop the convictions and the strength to do what is right. There's another way of life that is far better than drinking or drugs! When you make Christ your personal Lord and Savior, you can have power over the temptations.

I want to encourage Christian kids to remember that the greatest thing they have is their witness for Christ. As Christians, we should want to honor God, not just in what we say, but in our actions too. Our bodies are the temple of the Holy Spirit, and we don't want to put things in our bodies that are going to harm or destroy that temple. Alcohol and drugs can control us, but the Lord should be in control of our thoughts, decisions, and actions as believers.

Coaches may not believe this, but kids find out if they've been out drinking. The word gets around. Coaches think it will never get back to their players, but every high school player I know hears about his coach and knows when and where he goes out drinking. Coaches can be a really positive influence, and they can stress that drinking and drugs aren't going to help athletes perform. That'll only prevent them from doing their best.

Parents need to live what they want their kids to be. If you want your daughter to be a queen, Mother, then live like a queen. If you want your son to be a king, Father, then live like a king. Nobody is going to be perfect, but parents need to model what they want their kids to be.

MODEL EMOTIONAL STRENGTH

The best thing you can do for your son or daughter is be healthy yourself. No matter how many things you say, no matter how many good places you take them, no matter how much money you spend on them, the most important factor in your ability to help your teenager is your own emotional, relational, and spiritual example. It's also the hardest!

The same factors that affect troubled young people and that foster growth and healing also affect parents. The reasons teenagers deny the hurt or anger in their lives are the same reasons parents have for denying their own pain. What is sad is that parents have access to more resources than their children do, but don't take advantage of them to resolve their pain. They don't see them. They don't look for them. They feel helpless and hopeless that these resources will do any good. They feel stuck because of the following.

They get little support from their spouse. In fact, the spouse is often a source of pain, which leaves the one who wants help feeling oppressed, confused, and alone.

They are afraid of losing control over their feelings. Years of denying pain have served to control it. If they let these emotions surface, they are afraid they will erupt like Mount St. Helens!

They are afraid of being blamed for everybody's problems. People in the family probably have been blaming each other for every conceivable problem for years. If a parent has the courage to say, "I was wrong in some things I've said and done," she fears that everyone will use her as a blame dumping ground.

They are afraid of exposing "the family secret." What if somebody found out about the skeletons in the closet? What would they say? And how would the other family members react when they found out they had been betrayed?

They are afraid of being inadequate. "If my real problems surface," a parent fears, "I might not be able to handle them. Then I would have all the problems *plus* my shame *plus* the fact that somebody else knows about them. That's too much."

They aren't desperate enough to change. The main reason someone faces his or her inner wounds is this single factor: desperation. We cope, we play games, we hide, we deny, we do anything we can—until we simply *have to* face the reality and get the help we need. When we are desperate, we make the call for help. Not before.

Ironically, desperation is the door to hope. When we finally get going, we can learn to grieve, forgive, communicate, and build healthy behaviors. This is a long process for young people, and it's just as long for parents. But it's worth it. As we learn and grow, we will learn to model a positive character, listen, affirm, and provide a much healthier environment for our families.

MODEL CHARACTER

Rick was taking his eight-year-old son home from baseball practice. Little James was getting his notebook out of his backpack to see how much homework he needed to do that evening. The corner of the notebook snagged on the zipper, and it fell out of his hands. Papers flew out and fell in a mess on the floor of the car. "#@!" James said.*

Rick was shocked. He looked at his son for a few seconds, then said with disbelief, "What did you say?"

James looked at his dad and said confidently, "Well, you say it all the time!"

It may be a cliché, but it is true: Our children can't hear what we say because our actions speak so loudly! They watch what we do, and if what we do differs from what we say, we lose credibility in their eyes. As parents, we need to model the values we want our children to live by. Here are just a few areas we should examine:

Time and Money We may talk about being committed to God, the family, the church, or something else, but our *real* values show in our checkbook and daily schedule. The ways we spend our money and our time tell our children what is important to us.

Selection of Friends We can harp all day about the bums our children hang around, but we need to observe the friendships we model to them.

Language and Humor Paul encouraged the Christians in Ephesus to refrain from obscenity, foolish talk, and coarse jokes, and to focus instead on giving thanks (Eph. 5:4). Foul language, dirty jokes, racial slurs, and sarcastic statements can elicit a laugh or intimidate others. Either way, they teach our sons and daughters to talk and joke in the same way.

"Little" Decisions Our lives are filled with countless decisions that reflect our commitments, values, and discipline (or lack of) to our children. We set a bad example for them when we exceed our credit card limit, buy a car outside our budget, eat "just a little more" when we're on a diet, or watch television programs or movies that suggest that violence and premarital or extramarital sex are acceptable. One of the above may not make a big impact, but the pattern certainly communicates loudly and clearly.

LEARN TO LISTEN

We're tired. We've worked all day for a demanding boss. We didn't sleep all that well. The bills need to be paid, but there's not enough money in the checkbook. One child is late from practice, the other one won't do her homework. Your mother-in-law is angry because you didn't call last weekend. And you have a headache. Listening is about the four hundredth thing on your to-do list! But it is absolutely essential for a family's emotional health.

James encourages us to be slow to speak and quick to listen (James 1:19), but listening is hard work. One of the reasons listening is so difficult is that we sometimes feel out of control. We want to shape people up by telling them what to do! We don't want to listen to their excuses! But we need to realize that this motivation is self-focused. If we aren't good listeners (and you can tell that by whether people talk openly to you or not), then perhaps we need to examine our goals in communication: Is our goal to control others' behavior? To vent our frustrations? Or to affirm others and find workable solutions to problems?

Here are some principles of good listening.

Ask the second and third questions. When somebody tells you something, don't rush in with advice or condemnation. Ask follow-up questions to find out more. Perhaps you don't need any more information, but your questions will show that you care and that you are interested in the person, not just in fixing the problem. Instead of asking more questions, some of us interrupt with criticism, advice, and solutions. That sends a loud message to the other person to stop communicating.

Look beneath the words. Try to get the person to verbalize feelings, not just facts. Sometimes words communicate a confident message, but facial expression and tone of voice reveal insecurity and fear.

For instance, you may ask your son at dinner, "How are you doing?" He may respond by continuing to look at his plate and sadly saying, "Fine." If you respond only to his words, you will miss the reality of his condition. His girlfriend just told him she wants to date other boys. He's discouraged. He doesn't know if he ever wants another girlfriend if this is what it feels like. He probably doesn't want you to know about it because he doesn't want a lecture on "lots of fish in the sea." On the other hand, he'd be glad to know you think he's terrific.

It may be appropriate to say, "You look kind of 'unfine' to me. Is there anything you want to talk about?"

He may not say anything then, but you have opened the door to conversation. If this is your first attempt to really listen, you may not get very far until you have established a pattern of listening without fixing or condemning.

Ask for feedback. It is amazing that we can communicate as clearly as possible and still have others completely miss what we're trying to say. It happens all the time! If you have explained your feelings or values to someone, take the time to ask, "Now, I've said a lot. Maybe it's been confusing. What do you hear me saying?" The person's answer will tell you how clearly she's understood your message and your intentions.

In the same way, it is appropriate for you to give feedback to someone who is explaining something to you. You can say, "Thanks for telling me. Now let me tell you what I hear you saying, then you can fill in any parts I've missed."

Empower people to make their own decisions. One of the characteristics of an unhealthy family is when members make decisions for each other instead of letting others make their own choices. Changing this pattern is difficult, but essential. A woman who had controlled her husband and children with her domineering behavior was determined to change. She learned some communication skills, and soon, instead of telling others what to do, she said, "What are some options you can consider?" and "What would you advise someone in your situation to do?" and "I know I've told you what to do in the past, but I've been wrong. I hope you'll forgive me. Now we both have some adjusting to do: I need to keep my mouth shut, and you need to make your own decisions."

And she went one important step further. She said, "When you feel like I'm pressuring you to do what I want, please let me know. I may not want to hear it, but it will help me change. Will you do that for me?" Her husband and children almost fainted, but they liked being treated like people!

Give advice sparingly.   Advice is like a seed. If the ground is prepared through patient plowing, watering, and fertilizing, the seed will take root. But a farmer can sow thousands of seeds on parched, hard ground with very little success. Some of us sow far too many seeds of advice without taking the time and trouble to prepare people by listening to them. Much of that advice is ignored, and we become frustrated. And our solution is to give even more advice!

Sometimes we use advice to control others so that our lives are more comfortable. We use absolutes like *should*, *ought*, *always*, and *never*. One man realized he used these words to condemn and control his children. He determined to change, and he told his children, "I'm not going to 'should on you' any more!"

In his excellent book *Helping the Struggling Adolescent*, Dr. Les Parrott III suggests, "Advice will have more impact if it is not given routinely. Like a mailgram from Western Union, infrequent advice will stand out in importance."[1]

Listening is the key to giving advice that is accepted, because it earns the teenager's trust. If he doesn't trust you, even the most profound and accurate advice will be ignored.

FIND WHOLESOME ACTIVITIES

Some families enjoy doing all kinds of things together. Some go camping; some have long discussions about important topics; some congregate around sports activities; some play cards or chess or other games. But for many of us in strained relationships, it is difficult to envision these *Ozzie and Harriet* ways of relating to family members.

If the rapid pace of life, misplaced priorities, or ruptures in relationships make interaction difficult, don't try to bite off too much at once. Start small, look for common ground, and build on successes. For instance, if your son likes baseball, ask him if he thinks Ken Griffey Jr. is better than Barry Bonds. Ask a follow-up question or two, but don't try to dig too deep at first. When you watch a movie together, ask a few questions about the plot or characters. Don't try to do an *Entertainment Tonight* segment. Just ask a few questions and stop while the conversation is still good. Don't push it.

One way to stimulate conversation is to ask advice. "What do you think about . . . ?" is a good beginning to conversation. As this pattern builds rapport, it can be extended to activities, such as shopping together for a family member's birthday present, a trip to a ballgame, or a movie. Trust is built as opinions are valued. As trust grows, so do the opportunities for meaningful interaction.

SET REALISTIC EXPECTATIONS

"You don't understand!" is the adolescent's motto! Her desire for identity and freedom is often at odds with her parents' desires for her safety. If we fail to communicate our expectations of one another, we will create frustrations, anger, and even bitterness toward each other. Even when we establish clear expectations, they seem to change so often that it is difficult to know which way is right. But we need them for the sake of safety and sanity.

Expectations can change one way or the other based on the responsibility and maturity demonstrated by the adolescent. Generally, as he matures, he is given more freedom—as long as it isn't abused! Some of the issues parents and teens need to discuss are:

- curfews on weeknights
- curfews on weekends
- use of the car
- use of the phone
- allowance and other money matters
- dating policies
- television
- number of dinners with the family each week
- how summer vacation will be spent
- studying and grades
- household chores

Of course, any issue can be a potential sore spot if the adolescent and the parents have conflicting expectations. Expectations should be clearly stated so there are no misunderstandings. Flexibility, however, can be a part of the deal. For instance, a son may feel trapped because his parents only let him use the car one night each weekend. But they can tell him that if he doesn't have any trouble with the car and if he is willing to pay twenty-five dollars per month toward his car insurance, he can use the car more often. Rewards and consequences will help clarify expectations and motivate the child (and the parents!).

OFFER AFFIRMATION

"My daughter thrives on affirmation," a mother said with a look of amazement. "Her eyes light up. She sits up straight, and her whole countenance brightens!" This girl is not the only one. Campus Crusade for Christ speaker and author Ney Bailey says, "People live for encouragement—and they die without it."

Teenagers live in a cut-throat culture. They are either cool or uncool. If they are cool, they have to stay that way by saying the right things and being with the right people. Students are graded by teachers, and they are evaluated by coaches. But they are viewed microscopically by their peers and viciously condemned if they don't measure up. At school and in the neighborhood, they often live in an emotional desert. We need to ask ourselves, "Am I providing an affirming oasis for my family, or am I leaving them out in the desert?"

A father went to see a counselor about his son, who was smoking pot and missing school. The counselor asked him a strange question: "What are five positive qualities you see in your son?"

The dad stammered for a minute, then he said, "I don't see what this has to do with why I'm here."

"It has everything to do with it," stated the counselor.

The father named one quality, but he couldn't think of any others. "Okay, then," said the counselor, "what are five positive traits your son had when he was younger?"

The dad had an easier time listing his son's positive qualities as a child. "Well, let's see. He did pretty good in school. He used to do a really good job making model airplanes. He helped his Mom with the dishes without being asked. He and I went fishing and talked a lot. He was a lot of fun on those trips. Let's see. Oh, yeah, he used to draw really well too."

The counselor looked at him and asked, "And when was the last time you told your son you appreciated or liked something he did?"

The father bristled. "But I don't appreciate the way he's acting! That's why I'm here!"

"I understand that," the counselor stated calmly. "But his relationship with you is far more important than you can imagine. He desperately needs to hear his dad tell him he appreciates something—anything!—about him. But if you can't think of anything, you sure won't be telling him anything. You have to start thinking of things you like about him. It may be hard, but it's the start of rebuilding your relationship . . . and his life."

Angry thoughts feed angry behavior, which in turn feeds angry thoughts. This downward spiral continues until it destroys the desire to be together. Then it destroys the hope of a meaningful relationship. And finally, it distorts our every thought about the person. This cycle can be broken at any point by choosing to love unconditionally. That doesn't mean we deny the reality of the person's behavior or the hurt it can cause. It means we look that reality in the eye and say, "I love you anyway!"

Part of loving someone is looking for the good in your teen. His life may be so twisted by drugs or gambling or sex or something else that finding something good is difficult, but at least you can say, "Do you remember when we used to laugh and talk? It would mean a lot to me to have a relationship like that again. I know we can't go back, but we can start where we are and go forward. I love you. I want our relationship to be better, and I'm willing to work at it. Can we start over?"

As you begin to affirm your teen, you may be disappointed that you get little in return at first. Sometimes people, and especially teenagers, test you to see if your words are backed up by actions and attitudes. They want you to earn their trust. But sooner or later, you will reap what you sow.

UNCONDITIONAL LOVE

Unconditional love is a difficult concept for many of us. Some of us have controlled (or at least tried to control) others' behavior by fixing their problems. We feel good about ourselves when we feel needed. But in fact, fixing others' problems is really designed to fix our own need for appreciation. When we feel indispensable, we feel great! Our creed: "If they have a need, I'll meet it! If they have a little need, I'll make it into a big one, and then I'll meet it! If they don't have a need, I'll find one, and then I'll meet it!"

Fixing others' problems makes them dependent on us. It steals away their self-worth and confidence. Our overresponsibility makes them feel and act irresponsibly. They are accustomed to having us jump in and right every wrong and fix every problem. We are used to it too. This fixing feels like love to us because it looks like serving and giving. And being fixed feels like being loved because you are the recipient of someone's energy and thoughts. But fixing isn't love.

Fixing others' problems produces a rogues' gallery of emotions that doesn't remotely resemble love. If the person being fixed appreciates our efforts (and especially if others notice), we feel fantastically strong and heroic. We feel like the savior of the world (even though that job is already taken!) But when we fail or when someone doesn't appreciate our efforts, we feel self-pity and resentment. "I do *so much* for other people!" we lament. "And they don't even appreciate it."

Those we rescue also have conflicting emotions. If they have become dependent on us, they appreciate us, and indeed, are afraid of the thought that we would ever abandon them. But they resent the fixer's air of superiority. They may feel ashamed for being so helpless, and eventually, they may hate the one who helps them. This is often true in families where there is alcohol or drug abuse.

Change doesn't happen easily in these convoluted relationships. Setting expectations and administering consequences for irresponsible behavior has been avoided for years. But continuing down the path of dysfunction isn't the answer. It will only lead to more warped overresponsibility and irresponsibility.

Unconditional love is tough love. It means that we care enough to change our behavior for the good of another. It means that a fixer stops fixing and clearly communicates a commitment to let each person take responsibility for his or her own life and behavior. Tough love isn't a "hands off" approach at all. It requires careful consideration and planning, thorough communication, and tenacious follow-through with consequences.

The expectations outlined earlier in this chapter are a good place to start. Write them down. Negotiate the rewards, the consequences, and the flexibility (if any). And be sure to confess any wrong behavior that contributed to the problem. If you have been an overly responsible rescuer, admit it. If you have neglected the other person, admit it. Ask for forgiveness, and commit yourself to being appropriately responsible.

Very few (if any) of us can make these kinds of changes on our own. A wise pastor or counselor can give objectivity to your decisions. You will also need encouragement from others who have gone down the same path, so find a support group.

The course of change is rocky and rough, but it is possible. Remember, you can't make another person change. You can only invite him to change and set limits and consequences to shape his path. If he won't change, then you should consider an intervention like the one described in chapter 6. Get pastoral or professional help for this delicate and difficult task. It is often the last alternative for those who do not have the will to change on their own.

AND THE OTHERS TOO!

When a child is ruining his life on drugs or other addictions, our entire attention is focused on him or her. Sometimes our attention is so focused that we neglect others in the family.

When Barb was on the gymnastics team in high school, she developed anorexia. She was obsessed with being fit and trim. She ate very little, exercised for hours in addition to her grueling practices, and stepped on the scales a dozen times or more each day. By her sophomore year, Barb's friends were worried about her. She was eating less and less. They went to the coach.

After hearing the story from the girls, Coach Myers asked Barb to see her the next day after practice. Barb was shocked that anyone thought she had a problem. "I work my butt off, and this is what I get?" Barb cried as she angrily stomped out of the room.

After a few more attempts to talk to Barb, Coach Myers decided she needed to talk to Barb's parents. That meeting was no more pleasant than her talk with Barb. Barb's parents felt threatened by the coach's observations, and they were quite defensive. But after the coach cataloged Barb's behavior, Barb's mother finally began to recognize the pattern of anorexia and agreed to work with the coach to help her sick daughter.

Over the next two years, Barb was the focus of the entire family. But there was another child in the family—ten-year-old Carson. He under-

stood that his sister needed help, but he wondered why the only thing his parents could talk about was her. At first, he tried to continue talking to his dad about their favorite baseball team, but his dad would only explode with, "Carson, come on, son! Don't you know there are more important things in this family right now than box scores!?"

Carson got the message loud and clear. He got it often. And he got it continuously. It took three months for Barb to admit she had a problem, and it took over a year to begin to see changes in her eating behavior. By then, Carson felt like an orphan. He lived in the same house with Barb and his parents, but to him it seemed that his parents had only one child who mattered. Carson's problems would have been big enough if he had only had to deal with having a sister with anorexia, but his parents' neglect was a bigger problem by far.

When we must focus on one family member's problem, we need to be careful not to neglect others. Certainly we can focus attention on the critical need, but we don't have to create another crisis while we attempt to resolve the first one. Keep these principles in mind.

- Remember that any family member's problem is everybody's problem. See the family as an interrelated system.
- Have family meetings in which members can ask questions and discuss feelings. During this time, they can say anything they want without interruption. (You may need to have a two- to three-minute time limit.) If this liberty is abused, you may need to have some guidelines for communication styles. No subject, however, should be considered off-limits.
- Spend time with each individual in the family. Make eye contact, ask questions, and listen. You don't have to talk about the problem. In fact, it would be good to lighten up and talk about other things.
- Have regular reality checks. Ask yourself and each family member, "How are we doing? What can we do better? How can I help you?"

Most people realize that a wounded and broken family member needs more time and attention than the others, but all of them need at least *some* time and attention. Even more, they need the freedom and the invitation to say, "Hey, I need more!"

GETTING HELP

Feelings of helplessness and hopelessness are not the exclusive domain of the alcoholic or drug addict. Parents, siblings, and children of alcoholics and addicts feel that way too. All of them need help.

Some of us don't ask for help because we are so discouraged we don't believe anybody or anything can help us. Some of us don't ask for help because we don't want anybody to know how bad off we—or our families—are. Some of us don't ask for help because we've been told to handle our own problems. And we've complied, even when our lives were crashing around us. Some of us don't ask for help because we've asked before, and all we've gotten were quick, simple answers or condemnation for having the problem at all.

The body of Christ is meant to function in interdependence. Throughout the New Testament, the writers instructed members of the family of God to support each other by speaking the truth to each other in love, loving one another, accepting one another, and forgiving one another. Asking for help doesn't mean you are weak. It means you are objective enough to see your need and strong enough to do something about it. Strangely, we have no problem taking our car to the shop when it needs repairs. We don't hesitate to have our pants mended when they get torn. And we go to the doctor when we need surgery. In fact, we think there's something wrong with somebody who doesn't take the steps needed to fix a car, pants, or a torn anterior cruciate ligament. We need that same mentality when our families need to be repaired.

The difference, however, is the fact that our families are precious to us, and the problems which surface will probably be emotionally challenging to us. In other words, we're not sure we can stand it! In the family of God, pastors and counselors can help us apply the

Scriptures specifically and deeply. They can't promise results, but they are committed to helping us and our families experience the love and strength of God.

If you need help, don't hesitate to ask for it.

11

STAY IN THE GAME!

Harold Reynolds

California Angels

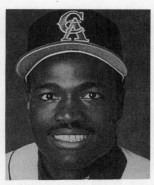

When I was a kid, I wasn't exposed to drinking or drugs. As I got older, I had already made my decision not to drink or use drugs. I already had enough natural high not to worry about getting high, and the greatest high I could possibly get came from God, the "High in the Sky!"

One of the biggest reasons why I didn't want to use drugs is that I wanted to be the best at whatever I did, and the only way to be your best is to be sober.

I always felt I was somewhat unique because I didn't use drugs and alcohol. I was different, and I liked being different. There were times in high school when I walked into a party and guys hid their beer and acted like they weren't drinking. And now that I've gotten older, when I go out and somebody asks me if I want a drink, I'll say, "I don't drink." They say, "Man, that's really admirable of you!"

When you can stand up for what you believe in, after a while, people know you are real, and they respect you.

Sports are full of stories of comebacks: Emil Zatapek running through his pain to win multiple gold medals in the Olympics, Arnold Palmer charging on the back nine on Sunday afternoon at the Masters, football teams down by thirteen points with two minutes to go pulling out a victory with two quick touchdowns, and (a real favorite) North Carolina beating Duke in basketball even though Duke was up by eight with only seventeen seconds left in the game!

Individuals and families make comebacks, too, but they usually don't make the front page of the sports section (or any other section). These battles are waged privately, away from the roar of the crowd. But they require every bit as much tenacity and determination.

A sign of a healthy family or a healthy team isn't perfection. That won't happen until we meet Jesus face to face. A sign of health is that we learn from our mistakes. We change, we adapt, we make hard decisions, and we make corrections so we can be more effective. That's why coaches wear headsets. They talk to their players during the game, giving instructions and correcting errors. That's why there's halftime!

It's the same with families and teams. We all make mistakes. We are rude, insensitive, controlling, demanding, or withdrawing. We need someone to say, "Hey! You can do better! Here's how." And we learn "new plays" in relating to each other. We learn to communicate better so we can have clearer expectations and anticipate others' moves. And we learn to win. But winning in relationships is different than being Number One. It means giving and loving and forgiving and talking even when (and especially when) you don't want to. There may be a thousand times we want to quit, but if we stay in the game, we can still win. You see, there's no time limit, no shot clock in family relationships.

Physiologically, muscles are built by putting them under stress. When the body repairs the resulting injuries, the muscles come back stronger than before. Nutrients and rest replenish the tissue. It's the same with character. Stress can make us stronger.

Ray had been in recovery from alcoholism for several months. He told a friend, "I always wanted to be strong and happy, but I would never have chosen this route to get there! The last few months have been the hardest I've ever experienced. I didn't know I could hurt so bad. At times it was awful! But you know, I didn't know life could be so good either. I thought I had friends before, but the friends I have now really care about me, not just about whether I can make them laugh. I thought I had a relationship with God before, but I was just playing games with Him. Now I'm learning—well, beginning to learn—what it means for Him to be my Heavenly Father. And I'm learning to be honest with myself about how I feel and the decisions I need to make. All this is hard. It's kind of like spring practice all day every day! But it's worth it."

No one can say for sure exactly why God allows things to happen in our lives. Sometimes we experience the consequences for our sins, like when we get a ticket for speeding, or when we flunk because we were high and didn't study. And sometimes we experience the consequences for other people's sins, like when a person runs a red light and hits us, or when a friend or parent's anger hurts us deeply. And sometimes we fall into self-perpetuation patterns of behavior. We keep making the same stupid mistakes over and over again. But no matter what the cause, we know that God can use our problems to build strength and character. We may not understand a lot of things about life, but we can be sure that God is sovereign, and God is good. He is the King of the universe, and He is a loving, compassionate, strong Father. Paul wrote to the Roman believers about God's use of difficulties in our lives.

We also glory in tribulations, knowing that tribulation produces perseverance; and perseverance, character; and character, hope.

Now hope does not disappoint, because the love of God has been poured out in our hearts by the Holy Spirit who was given to us. (Rom. 5:3–5)

God has a purpose for our suffering. It is to draw us closer to Him and to build our character. Others may have evil purposes in the way they treat us, but God's purposes are always for our good.

The Lord doesn't ask us to understand everything. He only asks us to believe that He understands everything. Proverb 3:5–6 says: "Trust in the LORD with all your heart, / And lean not on your own understanding; / In all your ways acknowledge Him, / And He shall direct your paths."

The process of growth doesn't just happen, just as the process of developing athletic talent doesn't just happen. It takes a clear mind and discipline.

SET REALISTIC GOALS

Whether you're a young person with a drug problem or a parent or coach of a troubled young person, you need to avoid the extremes of hopelessness and overconfidence. Hopelessness is easier, because you don't even have to try to make progress. But on the other end of the spectrum, people who are too confident often overlook the planning and preparation that are necessary to make good, life-changing decisions. Ask your counselor, pastor, youth minister, or group leader for suggestions as you work on your goals. Make your goals bite-sized and attainable, and enlist somebody to ask you about your progress on a regular basis. As you do the hard work of writing out your goals, here are some guidelines to consider.

- *Pressure points:* What situations and people are likely to cause difficulty? How will you avoid them?
- *Temptations*: How will you avoid the temptation to drink alcohol, use drugs, vent anger inappropriately, feel self-pity, or attack others?
- *Self-care*: When and what should you eat to get a balanced, healthy diet? What time do you need to get to bed to get eight

hours of sleep? What changes in your schedule (studying, television, chores, etc.) will have to be made to get to bed at that time?

- *Study*: What books do you need to read to enhance your progress? How much per day will you read? When? Will you keep a journal on what you have read?
- *God:* How can you develop you relationship with God? What passages or books of the Bible will you read? When? When will you pray? Will you keep a prayer diary to help and encourage you?
- *Encouragement and accountability:* Who will counsel you? How often? When?

Addicts and their family members often feel immobilized when it comes to goal setting. They are afraid to fail, and they are afraid that failure will spell disaster. Be realistic and flexible as you set goals. Realize that some may be more important than others. Also, be sure to get your counselor or group leader to give you feedback and encouragement about your progress.

HAVE REALISTIC EXPECTATIONS

People aren't machines. You don't just plug someone into the recovery process and watch things progress smoothly. There are predictable ups and downs. If we know these are coming, we won't be surprised by them. And we'll be more likely to know that we can get through them. Let's examine some common, predictable stages in the recovery process for both addicts and for their families.

Stage One It's almost uncanny. About a month after people see a counselor or go to a group for the first time, many of them feel very discouraged. One lady's experience is typical. She lamented in tears to her group, "I've been coming for a whole month now, and I thought that by this time, I'd feel better!"

Recovery opens a Pandora's Box of emotions. Much of the anger and hurt we have not allowed ourselves to feel suddenly become very real to us. We expected to feel better by this time. In this case, the old saying is true: "It gets worse before it gets better." Understanding the dynamics of this stage helps people realize they aren't going backward like they suspect. The feelings, horrible as they are, indicate that the person is making real progress. And yes, it will get better.

Stage Two   Progress brings the person to a deeper realization of his problems, and he is faced with difficult choices. He may realize that there is one thing he has never told anybody about—"the family secret"—and that he will get stuck if he doesn't talk about it and resolve it. Or he may realize that beneath all his anger are hurt and fear. Anger is a powerful emotion. It energizes. It motivates. Hurt and fear are very different. They make us feel vulnerable and weak. The person can stay stuck in his anger, or he can cross the abyss of and continue to make real progress.

By this stage, most people have much more understanding of what happened to them and why they feel so hurt and angry. But many (if not most) of them pursue the wrong solutions. They attempt to bargain—to swap attention, affection, or something else for the love they always wanted. "Now I know that my drinking was an attempt to block the pain of my parent's neglect," a woman told her counselor. Then she asked what seemed to her to be the logical question: "How can I get them to love me?" She wanted to swap something for her parent's love.

But bargaining isn't recovery. In fact, it is a roadblock to recovery, because it holds out a false hope that we can somehow control another person's behavior and get that person to give us what he or she has chosen not to give us in the past. Instead of bargaining, we need to grieve and forgive.

Stage Three   The choice to grieve our losses and forgive those who have hurt us causes us to face the stark, painful facts of those wounds—and those who have wounded us. We cannot grieve for something we deny or minimize. We won't see much need to forgive someone if "it didn't hurt that much." But when we are truly honest about our pain, we can then grieve our losses and forgive just as God has forgiven us.

At this important stage, we may choose to confront people about how they have hurt us. Facing an abuser or someone who neglected to give us the time and attention we needed is a traumatic experience which demands preparation. We recommend that you receive instruction from a counselor, pastor, or group leader before you proceed. Role plays are extremely helpful. In the case of someone who has died, is too sick to be confronted, or cannot be found, a counselor or group can let you confront a surrogate in a controlled situation. Here are some principles of confrontation.

Be prepared. Get input from others and write out exactly what you want to say.

Major on the majors. Don't talk about a hundred problems; focus on two or three. If these are resolved, you can bring up more later.

Set an agenda. State when and where you want to meet. At the meeting, take charge and say what you need to say. If you need to read it from your goal and preparation sheet, that's perfectly acceptable. The important thing is for you to accomplish your goals.

Clarify points. Ask questions like, "What do you hear me saying?"

Stay in control of yourself. Watch how you respond in the confrontation. If you wilt, sit up and speak out strongly. If you attack, calm down and lower your voice.

Don't expect instant repentance. Give the person a few days to respond to what you've said. That will let both of you be calmer in the confrontation, and it will be a truer measure of his or her response to you.

Anticipate the response. How does the person usually respond to stress like this? With self-pity? Anger? Blame? A combination?

Be patient. Don't expect to do this perfectly. Confrontation is a threatening experience for most of us, and we need the Lord's wisdom and strength to do it.[1]

Confronting those who have hurt us can be a springboard to healing in our own lives, and it can be the beginning of genuine reconciliation. Even if other people don't immediately respond positively—it can be a volatile situation—confrontation lets us see their hearts more accurately.

Stage Four   Throughout recovery, we learn new skills of communication and behavior. By this stage, these skills are taking a firm hold in our experience. The old patterns of wrong choices following wrong choices are gradually being replaced by new patterns. Our new friendships mean more than any before. We are more honest with ourselves and others. We can forgive, and we can ask to be forgiven when we blow it. Instead of playing games with people and trying to control them so they will meet our needs, we act like responsible adults.

Each of these stages includes critical decisions, and at each point we struggle with the choice to go on or not. Sometimes we wander off course for a few days, or a few weeks, or even a few months, but when we see the consequences of going back to the old ways, we become sufficiently desperate to get on the path again.

RELAPSE PREVENTION

It's a sad fact, but some people stray off the path and don't come back. What are some things we can do to avoid this? In chapter 7, we began to outline the recovery process. Those same principles help us stay on track after the process is begun. Let's look at how those apply to relapse prevention.

Self-Awareness   In Alcoholics Anonymous, people are made aware of potential relapse contributors with the acronym HALT, which stands for *hungry, angry, lonely, and tired*. When we experience these feelings, we are more susceptible to the temptation to drink, use drugs, attack, withdraw, or control people. In addition to those feelings, we need to be aware of times when:

- we feel hopeless and depressed. We feel like giving up, and we think it doesn't matter whether we drink or use or not.
- our thinking is distorted. We catch ourselves making black-or-

white, all-or-nothing, always-or-never statements. We exhibit grandiosity or paranoia, tunnel vision, delusional thinking, perfectionism, or indifference.

- we drift back into old relationships. Paul wrote the Corinthians, "Evil company corrupts good habits" (1 Cor. 15:33). When we hang around old friends, we are probably going to slip back into old patterns of behavior.

Triggers   What are the specific people and situations that give us trouble? We need to recognize those that trigger our reactions, and we also need to recognize the ones that encourage us to make good decisions.

Goals   In the first few weeks of recovery, we often experience a honeymoon period. Our goals are fresh and new. We feel challenged. But as the weeks and months go by, the drain and the constant discipline required to make good choices erode our enthusiasm. Our goals are filed in the drawer of the desk. But goals are important at every step of the process. We need to revise them periodically. Our needs change, and we need to be aware of the changes in our environment. Keep your goals current!

Boundaries   Some of our goals will spell out what we are responsible for—and what we're not. These are our boundaries. Progress or relapse is marked by our ability to define our boundaries clearly and stay within them.

Accountability   We probably didn't start on our own, and we don't get too far on our own either. We need encouragement (and sometimes a swift kick) from others who care enough to tell us the truth.

Recovery is hard work, maybe the hardest work someone has ever done, as one woman found out.

"But it shouldn't be this hard! I shouldn't have to put so much effort into it!" she lamented.

"You don't expect to be a good tennis player just by walking out on the court, do you?" said a friend, making a comparison to her favorite sport.

"Well, no." she paused. "But that's different."

"How is it different?" her friend persisted. "You practice a lot. You read tennis magazines. You take lessons. You talk to me about which grip to use on your backhand. You're committed to learning and improving. That's what it takes in both tennis and in recovery." She let it sink in a few seconds, then she concluded her sermonette, "The only difference is, tennis is just a game. Recovery is your life."

IT'S NEVER TOO LATE

The first time Kim walked into the church to attend a support group, she was petrified. She thought of a million reasons to turn around and walk away, but she knew she needed help. She took a deep breath and opened the door. The people in the room didn't look weird like she thought they would. In fact, she recognized several people. She was surprised to see them. "What are you doing in here?" she blurted to one of them.

Everybody laughed. They knew exactly how Kim felt, because they had felt the same way. "We're here for the same reason you are!" For a couple of weeks, Kim just listened. She had thought that she was the only one who had a son on drugs. She was afraid that she was the only one whose husband didn't understand her discouragement and fears. But now she realized she wasn't alone. She told the group, "When I walked through that door a few weeks ago, I was afraid that it was too late for me, too late for my son, too late to save my relationship with my husband. But now I see it's not too late. Your honesty and courage have given me hope that God can work—no, that He will work—miracles in our family!"

Throughout the Bible, we see proof that ours is a God of second chances for those who are willing to trust Him. The path is almost never easy, but those who follow can be assured that He knows the way. And in thousands of churches, support groups, Huddles, and counseling centers around the country, you can hear stories of brave men, women, and young people who know that God is still the God of second chances. It's never too late to let Him work in us and through us. He not only can, He wants to.

APPENDIX A

HOW TO START A FELLOWSHIP OF CHRISTIAN ATHLETES HUDDLE

Many people have asked how they can begin a Huddle. Here are answers to some questions people often ask us.

Question: What is the Fellowship of Christian Athletes?

Answer: The Fellowship of Christian Athletes is an interdenominational Christian organization that recently celebrated its fortieth anniversary. Its purpose is: *to present to athletes and coaches, and all whom they influence, the challenge and adventure of receiving Jesus Christ as Savior and Lord, serving Him in their relationships and in the fellowship of the church.*

Question: What are Huddles and why are they an important part of the Fellowship of Christian Athletes?

Answer: Huddles are the Fellowship of Christian Athletes groups initiated by student athletes. These groups are located on junior high, high school, college, and university campuses throughout the United States. Huddles are the backbone of the Fellowship of Christian Athletes' school-year program and give athletes a positive peer environment to encourage their Christian growth and service.

Huddles are designed for:

- Fellowship—Athletes experience a caring atmosphere and can seek a deeper relationship with Jesus Christ in this encouraging environment.
- Growth—Huddle leaders communicate biblical truths and encourage application and obedience in a wholesome, balanced lifestyle.
- Outreach—New people are invited to learn about Christ and experience the love and strength of His people by attending Huddles.

Question: Who can participate?

Answer: The Fellowship of Christian Athletes is targeted at athletes and coaches. Huddle participants are typically current or former members of recognized athletic teams and those who are vitally interested in athletics. However, the Huddle should not become exclusive or have a restricted membership. Our strategy is to target the coaches and athletes, but to welcome everyone they influence.

Question: Who can be a Huddle coach?

Answer: People who lead Huddles may be coaches, faculty members, or community volunteers. In addition to their desire to minister to student athletes, the most important criteria for Huddle coaches is a strong faith in Jesus Christ and a desire to follow Him.

Question: How can I obtain resources to be a Huddle coach?

Answer: The Fellowship of Christian Athletes can help. The Fellowship of Christian Athletes staff members, in or near most communities in the country, are available for consultation and support. In addition, we have many other resources, including:

- Huddle Resource Kit—Videos, meeting plans, personal encouragement, and much more.
- The Fellowship of Christian Athletes' *Playbook*—This handbook for the Fellowship of Christian Athletes leaders explains how to organize and facilitate a Huddle. The *Playbook* is a valuable resource for the coach and for student leaders.
- *Huddle Coach Network*—This monthly newsletter includes information, ideas, the Fellowship of Christian Athletes news, answers to difficult questions, encouragement for coaches, and a review of available resources.
- The Fellowship of Christian Athletes' Sports Shop—More than one hundred items of clothing, videos, books, and other merchandise are available by calling 1-800-289-0909.
- Insurance—As a Huddle coach, you will be covered under the Fellowship of Christian Athletes's liability insurance, and you will have the option to purchase Accident/Medical and Auto Insurance for Fellowship of Christian Athletes-sponsored events.
- Toll-free calling—You can call the Fellowship of Christian Athletes' toll-free number (1-800-289-0909) any time you want to contact the Home Office.

Question: How can I get started?

Answer: Good question! Here are some important steps:

1. Decide to start—Make a commitment to find the information and the leadership necessary, then get moving!

2. Select a Huddle coach and student leaders—There are actually two ways to start. A coach, an athletic coach, faculty member, or volunteer may have a vision for a Fellowship of Christian Athletes Huddle. This adult would serve as a sponsor for the Huddle. Or, students may have the initial vision. They can then find an adult to serve as the coach and sponsor. The school administration, however, needs to see that the Huddle is student-initiated and student-led, so mature, respected student athletes should form the leadership team.

3. Find supportive volunteers—Ask a group of coaches, teachers, parents, and volunteers to help the student leaders and the Huddle coach.

4. Ask for the administration's blessing—The student leaders and the coach should meet with the principal or other school officials to obtain approval for hanging Huddle posters and holding Huddle meetings on campus. The information in this section will help school officials understand your purposes.

5. Have an organizational meeting—Invite the coach, student leaders, and the volunteers to an organizational meeting to plan the Huddle schedule, content, materials, resources, and format. Be sure to invite the local Fellowship of Christian Athletes staff member. (Call the toll-free number to find the staff member in your area.)

6. Sanction your Huddle—Obtain a Huddle Registration Form from your Fellowship of Christian Athletes staff member. Complete it and mail it to the Home Office with your sanctioning fee. The Fellowship of Christian Athletes will then send you all of the resources and benefits previously listed.

7. Set a date—Find a time and place to meet, and get going! Meeting details and plans are included in the *Playbook*. Adults can help plan and coordinate the program, but the student should lead these meetings.

8. Call us any time you need us: 1-800-289-0909. We'll be glad to help any way we can!

APPENDIX B

GROUP LEADER'S GUIDE

This book is designed to be used individually or in groups. Coaches and group leaders can use its contents to communicate with young people, and parents' groups can use its contents for education and prevention. It can also be used as a tool for recovery.

IMPLEMENTATION STEPS

Your group can help youth live for Christ, drug- and alcohol-free! Here are four simple steps to follow to assure success.

Step One Read this book and understand the concepts.

Step Two Communicate the concepts of One Way 2 Play—Drug Free! to your group using the two meeting plans that follow these steps.

Step Three Ask people in your group to sign the commitment sheet (which is reproduced at the end of this Appendix). After they sign it, send a copy to the Fellowship of Christian Athletes Home Office at:

Fellowship of Christian Athletes
8701 Leeds Road
Kansas City, MO 64129-1680

We'd like to regularly publish the number of commitments made throughout the country. Display the commitment sheet in a prominent location to remind students of their commitment.

Step Four Reinforce the signers' commitment at least once a month by taking a couple of minutes to emphasize faith, commitment, and accountability. You may want to pair people and direct them to ask each other the questions listed on the commitment sheet, or you may want to have regular accountability partners. You may also want to ask these questions of each member of the group on an individual basis.

Note: the Fellowship of Christian Athletes offers many other resources, such as T-shirts, posters, bumper stickers, hats, and pins, which can help you with accountability. An order form is provided at the end of the book.

PLANS FOR TWO MEETINGS

As you prepare to implement One Way 2 Play—Drug Free! in your group, keep the following things in mind.

- The following two meetings are designed to be 30–45 minutes in length. Many people teach entire seminars on each of these subjects, so it probably won't be difficult to think of enough material to fill the available time. If the group is interested in continuing the discussion, take a few extra weeks to teach more principles and applications.

- The message is most powerful if the messenger has personal experience with its precepts. Take plenty of time to study, think about the message of One Way 2 Play—Drug Free! and apply the principles to your own situations and relationships. Personal illustrations will enable listeners to see how you relate to the information, and make them more likely to apply it themselves.

- Be real, but not too real! If you discuss your own past behavior, don't give sordid details. If you discuss someone else's sinful or embarrassing behavior, be sure to get permission or change the name and details so that the person's privacy is preserved.

- Remind group members: In the Christian life, we have to do our part, as God has to do His part (Phil. 2:12–13). We have the responsibility of responding actively to God's truth, and the Holy Spirit is responsible for strengthening and equipping us to do God's will.

- Tell the group how God can build their faith and provide a sense of stability and encouragement. Also, relate the previous to the importance of affirming and building up one another with respect and love.

- Let them know that if they want to talk further about deep hurts and needs in their lives, they can call you, the school counselor, their pastor or youth pastor, or someone else.

MEETING #1

Welcome Open the meeting with prayer. Greet the visitors. Follow with announcements of future meetings, special events, camp information, etc.

Warm-Up Divide people into groups of six to ten people. Give each group a piece of paper and a pencil. Ask each group to list celebrities (athletes, rock stars, actors, etc.) who died from drug overdoses. Then ask them to list celebrities who destroyed their careers, relationships, or health by using drugs.

After five to eight minutes, ask each group to share its answers, and give a prize to the group with the most names.

Workout Read the statistics on alcohol and drug abuse found in this book. Then explain that drugs and alcohol can ruin lives, friendships, and athletic performance. Briefly share a story or two from your own experience.

Divide those attending into groups again, and ask them to answer the following questions.

- What are some of the negative consequences of alcohol and drug abuse?
- What are some of the reasons people drink and use drugs?
- How can Christ give us the purpose, wisdom, and strength to live drug- and alcohol-free?

Let each group share its answers. If time runs short, focus on their answers to the last question.

Scripture Search Read and discuss with the group:

- Getting drunk (or high) is sin—Gal. 5:19–21
- Instead, be filled with the Spirit—Eph. 5:18
- Your body is a temple of the Holy Spirit—1 Cor. 6:19–20
- Don't cause others to stumble—Rom. 13:1–5
- All our choices, both positive and negative, have consequences—Gal. 6:7

Wrap-Up Close by asking each person to silently complete this prayer: "Lord Jesus, I want to live alcohol and drug-free because . . ."

Ask or assign four or five students to prepare a skit on the devastating effects of drinking and drug abuse. Call it "I Was a Teenage Morphine Power Ranger Pillhead." Ask them to interject humor, but conclude the skit with a powerful and serious message about the ways drugs and alcohol can affect family relationships, friendships, self-concept, motivations, and athletic performance.

MEETING #2

Welcome Open the meeting with prayer. Greet visitors. Follow with announcements of future meetings, special events, camp information, etc.

Warm-Up   Explain: "Last week we talked about the reasons people use alcohol and drugs, and the devastating consequences of using and drinking. To illustrate what we talked, we have a skit. And now, our not-ready-for-prime-time-players present: 'I Was a Teenage Morphine Power Ranger Pillhead.'"

The students should then perform.

Workout   Announce the planned event by saying "This week we are going to talk about what we, in our group, can do about alcohol and drug abuse."

Divide the attendees into small groups of six to ten people. Give each group a piece of paper and a pencil and ask them to answer the following questions.

- Why is it hard for many people to say no to drugs and alcohol?
- What are some specific ways we can help each other remain—or become—drug and alcohol-free?

Let each group share its answers.

Hold up the One Way 2 Play—Drug Free! commitment sheet and explain each component: faith, commitment, and accountability. Explain why and how each of these is important.

Divide them into groups again and ask them to write down their answers to these questions:

- What are some reasons you *wouldn't* want to make this commitment to Christ and to each other?
- What are some reasons you *would* want to make this commitment to Christ and to each other?

Let each group share its answers.

Explain that people who sign their names to a commitment are 60 percent more likely to keep that commitment, and that those who are in accountable relationships are 85 percent more likely to keep their commitments. Explain that you will display the commitment sheet at every Huddle or group meeting, and encourage those attending to ask each other these accountability questions on a regular basis (at least monthly). This can be done by assigning regular accountability partners. Or you, the coach or group leader, can ask them these questions.

Tell them you want them to come to the front to sign the commitment sheet. Before they come, lead them in prayer.

Allow time for people to come forward and sign the sheet.

After people have signed the sheet, show them the "accountability sign" of the index finger in the air. Say something like this: "This is the One Way 2 Play—Drug Free! accountability sign. Any time you see a brother or sister being tempted or making a bad choice to use alcohol or drugs, give them the sign as a reminder of their commitment. And if somebody gives you the sign, remember what you committed yourself to do and why you made your commitment. Help each other make the right choice and follow Christ in your actions."

Wrap-Up End the meeting by encouraging those attending to live for Christ, who loves them and will provide strength, wisdom, and love. Remind them you will ask them the accountability questions at your next meeting. Close in prayer.

SUGGESTIONS FOR LEADERS[1]

As you consider how you can lead your Huddle or group, think about these factors.

Seating Arrangement Ask everyone to sit in a semicircle so people can see each other's faces, especially during a discussion or sharing time.

Invite Disagreement Adolescents feel safer if they know you can accept their input without becoming defensive. Some young people say things just to see how you react. Try to affirm their contribution by saying, "That's a good question (or point). Thanks for telling us what you think." If the person's point is blatantly wrong, harmful, or unbiblical, you may need to add, "I'm glad you told us what you believe. Let me take this opportunity to tell you what I believe." Then graciously communicate your perspective.

Ask Good Questions There is an art to asking good questions. Learn to ask open-ended questions such as "Why?" "How would you feel and act if . . . ?" and "What are some ways we can apply this truth?" These questions stimulate reflection, discussion, and application.

Find Adult Helpers Recruit a coleader for your group or an assistant coach for your Huddle. (If you are a man, consider recruiting a woman to minister with you and focus attention on the young women.) The assistant leader or coach serves many important roles. They can:

- lead the group when you can't attend
- provide another set of eyes and ears to perceive the needs and opportunities in the group
- be a reality check for you as you bounce ideas and perceptions off group members
- provide lay counseling for those with particular needs

CHARACTERISTICS OF A DYNAMIC GROUP

Let's examine some of the characteristics of dynamic groups.

Love and acceptance Adolescents (and many adults) are experts at cutting people to shreds with sarcasm. They get a few laughs, but the victim is emotionally wounded and bleeding. It only takes a few sarcastic comments to create a tense mood. Energies are spent on getting revenge or hiding from attacks. This kind of environment is common among adolescents, but it destroys unity, love, and acceptance, which are vital to emotional and spiritual growth.

As the leader or coach, don't play this subtle but vicious verbal game with people in your group or on your team. Instead, model an attitude of unconditional acceptance. Remember that the teens are watching you. They may scoff when you don't join their fun, but as you continue to demonstrate gracious acceptance, they may join you in loving each other instead of cutting each other apart.

Your response to others' honesty will show how much you care. Don't feel that you have to solve every problem immediately. Listen carefully to people as they talk. Look at them. Ask them second and third follow-up questions to continue to draw them out. That will communicate that you really care about them. Also, use the ointment of thankfulness liberally. Say things like, "Thanks for telling us about your problem." Or "That took courage. Can we pray for you right now?" If someone shares something that needs your private attention, say, "Thank you for trusting us enough to tell us. Let's talk more about it after the meeting."

Trust Appropriate self-disclosure is one of the best ways to build an environment of trust. When you tell stories about your own failures, successes, hurts, fears, and hopes, others readily identify with you. Use self-disclosing statements such as, "I felt . . . when my parents divorced."

Encourage teens to talk about their dreams and dreads. As they feel safe, they will see how the truth you communicate applies to these areas of their lives. If someone shares information about a particularly abusive family situation, however, it is appropriate to gently interrupt and say, "Thank you so much for telling us about your hurts. I'm sure many people in here can identify with you. I'd like to talk more with you after the meeting. Do you have a few minutes to talk to me then?"

Information People are looking for truths they can apply to their relationships and experiences. As you teach, use quotes from books, the newspaper, and periodicals to add a punch to your talks. Personal illustrations or stories of others' experiences paint word pictures for listeners.

Too often, those of us who teach the Bible contribute to the perception that it's irrelevant because we don't relate its life-changing truths to our listeners. Help teens identify with the truth of the Scriptures by asking them open questions such as, "How would you have felt in this situation? What would you have done?" Or "What would Jesus do in this situation if He were here today?" Remember, you don't need to comment on the validity of each response. Simply thank each person for his or her contribution and summarize at the end.

Hope Many who observe today's adolescents call them the "hopeless generation." Their families are being torn apart. Their financial stability is shaken by strong but incomprehensible economic forces. The media encourages escape, but escape only heightens the sense of hopelessness. Your Huddle's environment of love, trust, and truth provides hope and encouragement. Think of times when you've felt confused and discouraged. When someone believed in you, you probably felt both surprised and strengthened! Young people (and adults) need to be reminded that the Lord is strong and loving. He loves them deeply and desires what's best for them. Though they may not understand their situation, He does.

Group leaders and coaches have the privilege of giving hope to these "hopeless" people.

- In the face of confusion, we can encourage them to make good decisions.
- In the face of weakness, we can help them to be strong.
- In the face of despair, we can tell them there is life on the other side of the present problem.
- In the face of guilt, we can share the forgiveness of Jesus Christ.
- In the face of bitterness, we can teach them to forgive others.

Be careful, however, not to overpromise! The Lord never promised to protect us or bail us out of all our problems. He promised to be with us in the middle of our struggles and to give us wisdom and strength to do His will.

Limitations There are limits to a leader's or a coach's training and time to deal effectively with the problems that surface in groups. Some mistakenly think they need to resolve every problem. This can lead to burnout. It can also lead to denial that there are any significant problems at all. Neither of these is productive.

We encourage you to find balance in this ministry. Here are some guidelines.

- Know your limitations. Be aware of the limits of your training, skills, and time to deal with complex individual and family problems.
- As you provide an environment in which people feel safe to talk about their hopes and fears, you can be sure that many of them will take the opportunity to talk! Be aware when the sharing is becoming too revealing for a large group. At that time, ask the person to talk with you privately after the meeting ends.
- If you assume the role of a counselor, you will need to determine when an adolescent's confidentiality needs to be maintained and when parents need to be informed. This is a difficult and tricky decision.
- We strongly recommend that you develop relationships with competent counselors and agencies in the community instead of playing a counselor's role yourself. These professionals are trained to handle the complex and dynamic struggles in individuals and families. You can ask to be informed of progress when a person is referred.

RECOMMENDATIONS

If you choose to use this book in a thirteen-week series, we recommend that you:

- Use the first meeting to communicate the goals of the group, to introduce people, and to acquaint everyone with the material. Have copies of the book available so that each person may buy one.
- Plan to cover a chapter each week. Of course, it is impossible to fully discuss each point in this short amount of time. You may need to schedule another thirteen-week series or an on-going group for those who want more depth.
- Recap what has been learned and discuss what the group wants to do next at the last meeting. Members may choose to disband, they may choose to continue, or they may split into two or more groups to address problems such as codependency, chemical dependency, or some other topic.

WE HAVE ACCEPTED THE CHALLENGE TO STRIVE FOR EXCELLENCE AS STUDENT ATHLETES BY CHOOSING THE ONE WAY 2 PLAY--DRUG-FREE LIFESTYLE!

FAITH IN JESUS CHRIST. WE BELIEVE CHRIST FORGIVES US, GIVES US THE WISDOM TO MAKE GOOD DECISION AND THE STRENGTH TO CARRY THEM OU

COMMITMENT TO SAY NO! TO ALCOHO AND OTHER DRUGS. WE PLEDGE TO BE STRONG IN OUR COMMITMENT AND TO HELP OTHERS BE STRONG, TOO.

ACCOUNTABILITY TO ONE ANOTHE WE WILL REGULARLY ASK EACH OTHER THE HARD QUESTIONS:

· ARE YOU LIVING AND PLAYING ALCOHOL AND DRUG-FREE?

· ARE YOU ENCOURAGING OTHERS TO LIVE AND PLAY THAT WAY?

· ARE YOU BEING HONEST WITH AT LEAST ONE MATURE PERSON ABOUT YOUR FEELINGS AND TEMPTATIONS?

· ARE YOU TRUSTING CHRIST TO MEET YOUR NEEDS?

· ARE YOU HONORING HIM IN YOUR THOUGHTS WORDS, AND ACTIONS?

_____

NAME OF FCA HUDDLE, SCHOOL, OR TEAM

_____ _____ _____
_____ _____ _____
_____ _____ _____
_____ _____ _____
_____ _____ _____
_____ _____ _____
_____ _____ _____

"ALL THINGS ARE POSSIBLE THROUGH CHRIST WHO STRENGTHS US." — PHILIPPIANS 4:

APPENDIX C

CRISIS COUNSELING

Almost every group includes people who have experienced significant stress and need more help than the group can provide. You may notice over the course of several weeks that an individual looks depressed or angry. When this happens, take a few minutes to ask the person what's going on.

Personal crises come in many varieties, and the symptoms and causes are often interrelated. Some of the causes of stress include:

- emotional problems—death of a family member or close friend, divorce, unresolved conflict
- abuse—physical, emotional, or sexual trauma inflicted by a spouse, sibling, family member, or acquaintance
- physical problems—disease, disability, or pregnancy
- change—marriage, childbirth, graduation, leaving home, divorce
- spiritual problems—unresolved guilt, bitterness, fear of or anger at God, purposelessness
- financial difficulties—unemployment, chronic poverty, disasters

When you find out that someone is in crisis, it is important to have a clear plan of action. Assess the situation, set specific goals, and intervene when it is appropriate. Let's examine the elements of this plan.

Assess the Situation

- What are the specifics of the problem?
- What personal resources are available (emotional, financial, and spiritual)?
- What is the person's ability to cope?
- What is the perceived loss?
- What is the perceived danger?
- How is the person interpreting the event?
- Are things getting worse or better?
- Is the person suicidal or homicidal?

Set Specific Goals

- Provide immediate "emotional first-aid."
- Decrease the person's anxiety level.
- Outline a plan to resolve problems.
- Instill a sense of hope.
- Identify additional resources.

Intervene

- Focus specifically on the current crisis, not vague ideas, feelings, or accusations.
- Encourage free expressions of feelings and thoughts.
- Involve others who can provide support.
- Teach crisis-management skills.
- Communicate biblical truth and principles about the crisis so the person can learn and grow.
- Use spiritual resources such as the Bible, prayer, the comfort of the Holy Spirit, and the encouragement of other believers.
- Understand the person's perception of the event and correct any false thinking, such as "I must have the approval of others to feel good about myself," "I am unworthy of love and deserve to be punished," or "I cannot change."
- Encourage the person to seek counseling from a trained professional.

Note: The Fellowship of Christian Athletes has developed a close relationship with Rapha Treatment Centers, one of the nation's leading providers of biblically sound, Christ-centered treatment for psychiatric problems and substance abuse. In hospitals and treatment centers across the country, Rapha offers a continuum of care for adults and adolescents, including books, seminars, intensive outpatient counseling, and partial and inpatient hospital care. Rapha has made their Information Counselors available to the Fellowship of Christian Athletes. If you need assistance as you try to help adolescents in crisis, please call Rapha to get professional direction. Their number is 1-800-383-HOPE.

ENDNOTES

Chapter 1

1. H. Stephen Glenn and Jane Nelsen, eds., *Raising Self-Reliant Children in a Self-Indulgent World* (Rocklin, CA: Prima Publishing and Communications, 1989), 30-31.
2. Charles Colson, *Against the Night* (Ann Arbor, MI: Servant, 1989), 74-75.
3. The American Council for Drug Education, *News Release*, Rockville, MD, 1994.
4. Tom Parker, *In One Day: The Things Americans Do in a Day* (Boston, MA: Houghton Mifflin Co., 1984), 31.
5. *The 1993 Almanac* (Boston, MA: Houghton Mifflin Co., 1993), 456-68; and *Facts on Alcoholism and Alcohol-Related Problems* (New York, NY: National Council on Alcoholism, 1988), 6.
6. The American Council for Drug Education, *News Release*.
7. Josh McDowell, *Why Wait?* (Nashville, TN: Thomas Nelson, 1987).
8. Parker, *In One Day*, 31.

Chapter 2

1. *The 1993 Almanac*, 468.
2. D. W. Goodwin, "Alcoholism and Heredity: A Review and Hypothesis," *Archives of General Psychiatry*, 36 (1979), 57-61.
3. Bob Welch, *More to Life than Having It All* (Eugene, OR: Harvest House, 1992).
4. Jerry Johnston, *It's Killing Our Kids: The Growing Epidemic of Teenage Alcohol Abuse and Addiction* (Waco, TX: Word, 1991).
5. American Crisis Publicity Company, *Americans for a Drug-Free America*, Austin, TX, 1991.
6. Mickey Herskowitz, "The book on Lucas? Winner a day at a time," *Houston Post*, 14 September 1994.

Chapter 3

1. René A. Spitz, "Hospitalization: An Inquiry into the Genesis of Psychiatric Conditions in Early Childhood," *The Psychoanalytic Study of the Child*, Vol. 1 (New York, NY: International Universities Press, 1945), 53-74.

2. Dr. Les Parrott III, Rapha seminar "Excellence in Pastoral Counseling," Houston, TX, April 1994.
3. The American Council for Drug Education, *News Release*.
4. Sharon Wegscheider-Cruse, *The Family Trap* (out of print), and Dan Allender, *The Wounded Heart* (Colorado Springs, CO: NavPress, 1990).

Chapter 4

1. Stephen Arterburn and Jim Burns, *Drug-Proof Your Kids* (Pomona, CA: Focus on the Family Press, 1989).
2. Les Parrott III, *Helping the Struggling Adolescent*, (Grand Rapids, MI: Zondervan, 1993), 93.
3. The American Council for Drug Education, *News Release*.
4. Parrott, 97.
5. "Facts about Drug Use and HIV/AIDS," Centers for Disease Control, September 1993.
6. The American Council for Drug Education, *News Release*.
7. Ibid.
8. John Q. Baucom, *Help Your Children Say No to Drugs* (Grand Rapids, MI: Zondervan, 1987), 130-31.
9. "More teens using drugs, survey says," *Houston Post*, 20 October 1994.
10. Ibid.
11. Parrott, 96.
12. The American Council for Drug Education, *News Release*.
13. Charles E. Yesalis, *Anabolic Steroids in Sports and Exercise* (Champaign, IL: Human Kinetics Publishers, 1993), 41-42, 314.

Chapter 5

1. Robert McGee, Pat Springle, and Tom Joiner, *Rapha's Twelve-Step Program for Overcoming Chemical Dependency* (Dallas/Houston, TX: Word/Rapha, 1991).
2. Robert McGee, Stuart Rothberg, and Pat Springle, *How to Tell If Someone Is on Drugs* (Houston, TX: Rapha, 1994).
3. American Psychiatric Association, *Diagnostic and Statistical Manual of Mental Disorders*, 3rd rev. ed. (Washington, D.C.: American Psychiatric Association, 1987).
4. Ibid.
5. Parrott, 95.
6. G. Beschner, "Understanding Teenage Drug Use," *Teen Drug Use* (Lexington, MA: Health, 1986).
7. Adapted from the Johns Hopkins Questionnaire.
8. Adapted from an ACOA questionnaire.

Chapter 6

1. Gary Collins, *Christian Counseling* (Dallas, TX: Word, 1988).
2. Adapted from *Rapha's Liability Management Notebook for Pastoral Counselors* (Houston, TX: Rapha, 1994).
3. J. L. White, *The Troubled Adolescent* (New York, NY: Pergamon, 1989).

Chapter 8

1. *Sharing the Victory* (Fellowship of Christian Athletes magazine), May/June 1989.
1. Information sheet from The Crestview Center, Anderson, IN.

Chapter 10

1. Parrott, 39.

Chapter 11

1. Pat Springle, *Trusting: Knowing Who and How to Trust Again* (Ann Arbor, MI: Vine Press, 1994), 156-61.

Appendix B

1. Richard Price and Pat Springle, *Rapha's Handbook for Group Leaders* (Houston, TX: Rapha, 1992), 51-64.

ABOUT THE AUTHORS

Dal Shealy has been President of Fellowship of Christian Athletes since June of 1992. He came to FCA from the University of Richmond in Virginia, where he was head football coach of the Spiders. He has been involved in organized football for thirty-nine years as a player, coach, and motivator of young athletes. He is also an author, inventor, and national speaker at clinics, banquets, seminars, churches, and conventions. Dal has been active in the Fellowship of Christian Athletes since the mid-sixties. He and his wife, Barbara, have three children and five grandsons and live in Liberty, Missouri.

Pat Springle has an M.A. in Counseling. He served with Campus Crusade for Christ for eighteen years, eleven of them as the Texas Area Director. He also served as Senior Vice President for Rapha for three years and has served as a consultant for Fellowship of Christian Athletes. Pat has written several books, including *Trusting: Knowing Who and How to Trust Again, Codependency: A Christian Perspective, Rapha 12-Steps for Overcoming Codependency,* and coauthored several, such as *Your Parents and You, Getting Unstuck,* and *Rapha's Handbook for Group Leaders.* He and his wife, Joyce, and their two children, Catherine and Taylor, live in Friendswood, Texas, where Pat is President of Baxter Press.

RESOURCES

HAT
Cost - $ 12.00 / Order #A1035

PATCH

2.5"X3.5"
For Letter Jacket or Uniform
Cost - $ 1.50 / Order #A7503

SIDE 1

SIDE 2

KEYCHAIN
Cost - $ 1.50
Order #A7501

BACK

FRONT

SHIRT
: L, XL, XXL
st - $12.00
er #A2120

I'M PLAYING DRUG-FREE!

BUMPER STICKER
Cost - 50¢ / Order #A7502

VIDEOS FOR YOUR GROUP!

CHOICES, THE CHIP CUOZZO STORY—Chip Cuozzo, was a gifted athlete — In Choices, his family shares their eyewitness accounts of Chip's struggle to find identity and purpose in today's world, and the hope we can all find if we make the ultimate choice in life. Cost $19.95. Order #TV040.

ALONE IN THE DARK is a 27-minute science fiction thriller dealing with teenage drinking and driving, and the surprise ending involves the viewing audience's participation. A study guide based on Biblical principles is available. Cost $30.00. Order #TVO39.

OSTER
22" - Bright Colors
: - $2.00
er #A7504

**FOR MORE INFORMATION
OR TO PLACE AN ORDER, CALL
1-800-289-0909**

ORDER FORM

ONE WAY
2 PLAY

DRUG FREE

NAME _____

PHONE: DAY(_____)_____

         EVENING (_____)_____

SHIPPING ADDRESS_____

CITY_____STATE_____ZIP_____

Order #	Size	Item Description	Quantity	Price	Total

**SHIPPING CHARGES

$1.00 - $25.00 ....$3.50
$25.01 - $50.00 ....$4.50
$50.01 - $100.00 ....$5.50
$100.01 - $250.00 ....$7.50
$250.01 - $400.00 ....$10.00
over $400.01 ....FREE

Merchandise Total	
Shipping and Handling**	
ORDER TOTAL	

METHOD OF PAYMENT

❏ Check or money order
    enclosed payable to:
    FCA

❏ VISA   ❏ Mastercard

Expires_____

Card Number

TOLL-FREE ORDERING
for credit card holders:
1-800-289-0909
or (816)921-0909 (in KC area)
(8:00 a.m.- 4:00 p.m. Central Time)

Signature _____

Date _____